# POMEGRANAT

## Ann Kleinberg

*Photography by Josef Salis*

**TEN SPEED PRESS**
Berkeley | Toronto

A Kirsty Melville Book

Ten Speed Press
P.O. Box 7123
Berkeley, California 94707

Distributed in Australia by Simon and Schuster Australia, in Canada by Ten Speed
Press Canada, in New Zealand by Southern Publishers Group, in South Africa by
Real Books, and in the United Kingdom and Europe by Airlift Book Company.

Cover and Interior Design by Michel Opatowski

Library of Congress Cataloging-in-Publication Data
is on file with publisher

ISBN 1-58008-631-4

First printing, 2004

Printed in Hong Kong

1 2 3 4 5 6 7 8 9 10 - 06 05 04

# Contents

*Acknowledgments*
4

*The Pomegranate—An Extraordinary Gift from Nature*
6

*From Orchard to Table*
10

*Starters & Soups*
20

*Salads & Side Dishes*
44

*Main Courses*
64

*Desserts & Drinks*
88

# Acknowledgments

The writing of this book has led me on an incredible journey—to develop and compile a collection of recipes into a single-subject cookbook on pomegranates, a feat never before undertaken (to my knowledge). I was daunted, but determined. Once people got over the initial surprise ("What could you possibly write about pomegranates?"), they were incredibly helpful. "Well, come to think of it, my grandmother used to make pomegranate juice, and she made us drink it to stay healthy." "You know, I remember my aunt had a recipe in her tattered cookbook for chicken with pomegranates and walnuts." And so it flowed. And so flows my gratitude—as plentiful as the seeds of a pomegranate.

To Nizza Ben Shalom, my friend and culinary mentor, there are no words to express my appreciation. Without her enthusiasm and professional kitchen wisdom, this book might never have made it to the shelves. She tested, tasted, and tweaked from her restaurant Boccaccio in Tel Aviv to my kitchen in Caesarea—always inventing and suggesting. Her chef, Eran Drori, and her mother, Reena Ezra, also offered some of their cooking magic.

Linda Zaga, whose knowledge of Syrian cuisine is inspiring, transformed those pomegranate seeds into one incredible dish after another. Her pomegranate molasses is like no other I have ever tasted! Many thanks are due her and her daughter Sefi Kerem, who happily joined the project and translated her mother's "just a handful" into book-worthy measurements.

Eysar Horesh, my Persian food consultant, shared her cooking skills, provided critical tips, and kept me going when deadlines and pomegranate mania were about to take over. Gabriel Shachar, head chef of Jerusalem's King David Hotel, whipped up some wonderful dishes as well as ideas, providing the perfect jump start.

To Shelley Goldman, who gave me my start in food writing and pushed me to keep going, I am eternally grateful. To Rachel and Elan Penn, my publishers, who were willing to take a chance—what a pleasure it has been working with them. Thanks are also due Niv Agriculture and Kibbutz Gan Shmuel, who kept me in pomegranates when they had all but disappeared from the shelves.

There have been so many wonderful teachers, gifted authors, and talented chefs I have learned from and been inspired by—each has contributed to my love of preparing, eating, and writing about food.

To the friends who offered a recipe, lent a book, or just put up with my obsession with pomegranates—I am so very grateful. And most especially to the pome of my soul—O.P. He encouraged the writing, sampled the food, and happily lived with this passion for pomegranates. Thank you from the bottom of my heart.

Ann Kleinberg

# The Pomegranate
## An Extraordinary Gift from Nature

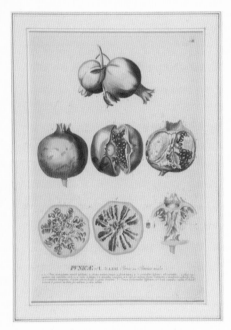

Georg Wolffgang Knorr, etching on paper, 1751, private collection

The pomegranate—regal, luscious, and delicious. How does one introduce this extraordinary fruit and pay homage to its noble heritage? For this is no food of mere mortals—this is a food of the gods, with a history resplendent in legend and lore.

The crown-topped pomegranate has suddenly become the darling of the Western dining table, its newfound popularity propelling it to celebrity status. Television has featured it (in lifestyle shows, cooking programs, and even a cameo appearance on *Sex and the City*), the print media has devoured it (from Oprah Winfrey's O to *Time* magazine), and chefs from the East Coast to the West are flavoring their foods with it. The pomegranate is the new food of the new millennium. Wouldn't King Tutan-khamen be having a good laugh over this—he was buried with pomegranates thousands of years ago!

The truth is, pomegranates have been around forever. The Old Testament, for instance, is rife with pomegranate references—from allusions of love: "Let us go early to the vineyards . . . and if the pomegranates are in bloom—there I will give you my love" (Song of Solomon 7:12), to symbols of ornament: "On the capitals of both pillars . . . were the two hundred pomegranates in rows all around" (1 Kings 7:20), and imagery of hope: the Promised Land to which Moses led his people was said to be "a land with wheat and barley, vines and fig trees, pomegranates, olive oil and honey" (Deuteronomy 8:8).

And while we are on the subject of the Bible, can we even be sure that it was an apple with which Eve enticed Adam? Apparently not, because many scholars believe that the fruit of temptation, leading to banishment from the Garden of Eden, was none other than the pomegranate. What a juicy tidbit to consider!

The allure of the pomegranate has captured cultures throughout history, both real and imaginary. The ancient Egyptians included pomegranates in their tombs, to ensure safe passage to the next world and rebirth. Greek myth attributed the arrival of winter to Persephone and her inability to resist the luscious pomegranate. The Chinese gave wedding gifts with images of pomegranates to promote a fruitful union. Understandably, the round shape and myriad seeds have come to represent fertility and bounty. And to this day, Jews honor the fruit by including it in the festive meals associated with Rosh Hashanah, the Jewish New Year.

The pomegranate image has figured prominently in art throughout the ages. It appears in the paintings of artists as diverse as Caravaggio and John Singer Sargent. The religious imagery evoked by the fruit is significant—Botticelli placed a pomegranate in the hand of baby Jesus in his painting *Madonna of the Pomegranate* (Uffizi Gallery, Florence), and the meaning of the "bleeding" pomegranate tree in the *Unicorn Tapestries* of the fifteenth century (Metropolitan Museum of Art at the Cloisters, New York) is still a debated topic.

The pomegranate is absolutely captivating. The fullness of its form, the leathery skin in shades of gold to burnished red, the crowned peak and hairy antennae hiding within—the fruit seduces one to pick it up and caress it. Many admirers have been sufficiently mesmerized by the pomegranate to use it for ornament alone.

Beyond all the pomegranate's glamour, and way beyond its current fifteen minutes of fame, the most important feature of this marvelous food is that it offers an oasis of health benefits. Results of ongoing medical research indicate evidence of significant antioxidant and antiviral activity. There is great hope that the inherent properties of the pomegranate may in the not-too-distant future be helpful in breast cancer treatment and hormone replacement therapy.

While folk medicine has long promoted the pomegranate—finding uses for the juice, seeds, and rind to treat illnesses ranging from sore throats to dysentery—the recent spate of attention has caused scientists to clear off their counters and bring on the pomegranates. Forget red wine and green tea—the healthy benefits to the cardiovascular system from pomegranate juice far outweigh all the other drinks. Even the cosmetic industry has exploited the astringent properties of the pomegranate, using it in soaps, shampoos, body scrubs, and creams. And lest we forget, the pomegranate has often been thought of as an aphrodisiac.

The fruit, whose Latin name is *Punica granatum*, originated in Persia and has been cultivated throughout the Mediterranean region. This "many-seeded apple," which thrives in a climate of mild temperature and low humidity, is found in Africa, India, the Near East, and southern Europe. In the eighteenth century, the pomegranate arrived in America—brought by the Spanish—where currently it is grown in California and the southern United States. Origin of the words "grenade" and "garnet," the pomegranate is even the namesake of the Spanish city Granada. At last, the world has become pomegranate-savvy, and this extraordinary food is claiming its rightful place on the table.

Romance and science aside, pomegranates taste great. Those little kernels of seed surrounded by flavorful scarlet flesh (called arils) are a delightful addition to all kinds of dishes. Whether used as a garnish, as a drink, or in concentrated syrup form as an integral part of a dish's composition, pomegranates add beauty and stimulating flavor.

*Pomegranates* presents a collection of recipes from starters to desserts, all made with pomegranates. Descriptions of how to select and store the fruits, open them, and cook with them are offered in user-friendly, uncomplicated language. The emphasis in this book is on healthy ingredients that are commonly available, though once in a while an exotic spice or combination of flavors is sprinkled in. Some dishes are based on traditional ethnic cuisine, such as the Persian-inspired Walnut, Date, and Pomegranate Chicken; other dishes are modern variations, such as Spareribs in Pomegranate Barbecue Sauce.

For hors d'oeuvres you might be tempted by Drunken Figs with Roquefort in Pomegranate Syrup or the Pomegranate Guacamole. For the next course you could choose Beet and Pomegranate Borscht or the Salmon Gravlax with Pomegranate Balsamic Dressing. If you're in the mood for Middle Eastern, then you must try the Meat, Pine Nut, and Pomegranate Pastries. If an appetite for Asian strikes you, the Tuna, Asparagus, and Pomegranate Stir-Fry can be ready in a few minutes. And for dessert, choose from recipes for sorbets, napoleon, rice pudding, and even mixed drinks—without a doubt, there's a pomegranate extravaganza for the sweet tooth in everyone.

Whether you read *Pomegranates* from cover to cover, or jump right in and start cooking with pomegranates, I wish you joy on this delicious journey. May you have as many successes as the seeds of a pomegranate.

# From Orchard to Table

*How to Select and Store a Pomegranate*

*How to Juice a Pomegranate*

*How to Seed a Pomegranate*

*Basic Recipes*

Pomegranate Syrup

Pomegranate Molasses

Basic Vinaigrette with Pomegranate Juice

Basic Vinaigrette with Pomegranate Syrup

Mixed Berry and Pomegranate Coulis

## How to Select and Store a Pomegranate

Pomegranates are a seasonal fruit, appearing in the markets during the autumn months. They have a brief harvest time beginning in late summer, but their shelf life is long and you can usually find them through December.

Picking a pomegranate is easy, because there is very little that can go wrong with it. The rind is tough, which protects the fruit from harm. Look for pomegranates that are heavy, without any blemishes, cracks, or soft spots. They should be firm to the touch and mostly red in color.

Store pomegranates in the refrigerator, sealed in a plastic bag if not using right away (this helps retain their moisture).

---

## How to Juice a Pomegranate

An average pomegranate yields about $1/2$ cup juice.

Refrigerate and use within 2 days.

**Method 1:** Roll the pomegranate around on the counter—this will help get the juice out. Cut off the crown end. Cut the fruit in half and place one half in a hand-operated citrus juicer (do not try this with an electric juicer—it may squirt the juice all over the place). With a strong arm motion, bring down the handle and squeeze out the juice. Repeat with the remaining half. If the fruit is large, cut it into quarters and squeeze each section. There is waste with this method, but it is the easier way.

**Method 2:** Follow the instructions for seeding the fruit (see next page) and then process the seeds in a blender or food processor or pass them through a food mill. Strain the juice through a cheese-cloth-lined mesh sieve so that you are left with only the juice and none of the tough parts.

# How to Seed a Pomegranate

An average pomegranate yields about ³/₄ cup seeds.

Refrigerate for 1–2 weeks, or freeze for up to 6 months.

This is going to be fun—well, maybe not the first time—but once you get the hang of it you may make it a daily ritual. Consider wearing an apron for your first seeding adventure.

Two things to keep in mind: yes, you can eat the seeds, and no, there is no definite number of seeds per fruit. Depending on the variety, the larger the fruit, the more seeds it contains.

It's best to undertake this operation while standing over a sink. And if you have a large bowl (plastic works great) with a colander that fits inside, you're all set.

Cut off the crown end of the pomegranate, slicing close to the edge of the rind and trying not to damage the seeds inside. Score the rind from top to bottom all the way around, creating four or five sections, but do not let the knife penetrate to the inside. Using both thumbs to secure the bottom of the pomegranate, wrap your hands around the fruit with your fingers at the cut crown end and pull the sections apart. Be careful—this is when it tends to squirt, so make sure that the opening faces down into the colander.

Some of the seeds will fall out naturally. Others will need a bit of coaxing. The next step requires a bit of patience. Hold a section of fruit, pull out a cluster of seeds (which are encased in a honey-comb of pith that looks and feels like tissue paper), and coax the seeds out with your fingers. Repeat with the remaining clusters of seeds.

If you want to have more fun, take a wooden meat pounder or large spoon and, while holding the section with the cut side facing the palm of your hand, give a couple of whacks to the back of the pomegranate (take care that you don't hit your hand!). That should be enough to send those seeds hurtling right into the colander.

Once all the seeds are in the colander, you will inevitably find some pieces of pith among them. The best way to remove these is to fill up the bowl with enough water to cover the seeds. The bits of pith will naturally float to the top and the seeds will sink to the bottom. Using a slotted spoon, scoop up and discard all the little white pieces. Then pick up the colander, letting the water drain out, so that you are left with just the seeds.

Pomegranate seeds will keep in the refrigerator for 1 to 2 weeks and in the freezer for 6 months. For either way, spread them out on a flat tray or put them in a plastic bag, cover the tray with plastic wrap or seal the bag, and refrigerate or freeze. Once frozen and thawed, use immediately—thawed seeds have a tendency to bleed and disintegrate when rechilled.

---

# Basic Recipes

Since the explosion of pomegranate mania, products that were previously unavailable are suddenly showing up in food markets. When purchasing them, however, a word to the wise is in order. Many are imported and there is no "standard of the industry" regarding names and ingredients. You may find products referred to randomly as syrup, molasses, paste, nectar, and concentrate, all containing the same thing. Some have sugar and preservatives added, while others are pure and 100% natural. Grenadine, for instance, long ago forfeited any authentic association with the pomegranate fruit for which it was named, yet it may still be touted as a pomegranate flavoring.

# Pomegranate Syrup

*Making your own pomegranate syrup is well worth the effort—the taste is remarkable.*
*If you have the time and inclination, go for it.*

4 cups pomegranate juice

Makes about 2 cups

When making pomegranate syrup, you can use freshly squeezed or store-bought pomegranate juice (buy only pure juice, without sugar or flavorings added). You will need a large amount to start with; try it with 4 cups as there is a lot of evaporation in the cooking process. Depending on how thick you like your syrup, 4 cups of juice will reduce to yield about 2 cups of syrup.

Pour the juice into a saucepan or skillet and bring to a steady boil over high heat. Decrease the heat to maintain a steady, low bubbling, and cook, stirring occasionally with a wooden spoon. After about 20 to 30 minutes the juice will have reduced by about one-half and will start to thicken.

To test consistency, dip a spoon in the syrup—if it comes out relatively clean, continue cooking. If the spoon is coated and the syrup takes its time about sliding off, you've done it! Another method is to drop a spoonful of the syrup on a chilled plate and wait a few minutes (or place the plate of syrup in the refrigerator to hasten the process). If the syrup moves slowly around on the plate, that's it—remove the pan from the heat and let cool completely. If it is still runny, continue cooking but pay close attention at this point. If you want very thick syrup, continue cooking and then remove from the heat when the syrup reaches the desired consistency or even a little before—it will thicken as it cools.

Pour the cooled syrup into a jar and close tightly. It will keep in the refrigerator for 6 months.

# Pomegranate Molasses

*Making pomegranate molasses is similar to making syrup—it just requires more time and the addition of sugar and citric acid (sometimes called sour salt) or lemon juice. It may take some practice, but don't give up—the taste is spectacular. Try it spread on bread, drizzled over cakes, or poured over waffles.*

---

4 cups pomegranate juice plus additional
    if needed

4 cups sugar

1 to 3 tablespoons citric acid or freshly
    squeezed lemon juice

Makes about 4 cups

Pour the pomegranate juice into a saucepan and bring to a steady boil over high heat. Decrease the heat to medium-low and gradually add the sugar, stirring to dissolve it. Adjust the heat to maintain a constant simmer.

Keep your eye on the saucepan, watching closely for the transformation to syrup consistency to begin (see previous page). At the very first indication of thickening, stir in 1 tablespoon of the citric acid and taste. If you prefer a more tart flavor, add another 1 to 2 tablespoons of citric acid.

When the mixture starts to resemble syrup, test it for doneness. Drop a spoonful on a chilled plate and wait a few minutes (or place the plate in the refrigerator to hasten the process). If the molasses is somewhat sticky and moves slowly around on the plate, it's done—remove the pan from the heat and let cool completely. If it is still runny, continue cooking.

The trick to molasses success is in knowing when to take it off the heat. Molasses can easily burn if cooked over too high a heat, or it can harden into taffy if cooked too long. Keep in mind that the molasses will set even further as it cools. To be on the safe side, stop cooking before it reaches the desired consistency. If the mixture is too thick, dilute it with additional pomegranate juice and reheat.

Pour the cooled molasses into jars and close tightly. It will keep in the refrigerator for 6 months.

# Basic Vinaigrette with Pomegranate Juice

*Before dressing a salad, it is always a good idea to rinse the greens well and dry them in a lettuce spinner or pat them dry with absorbent towels. Do the same for fruits and vegetables.*

$1/4$ cup pomegranate juice

3 tablespoons white wine vinegar

3 tablespoons extra-virgin olive oil

2 tablespoons canola oil

1 tablespoon freshly squeezed lemon juice

4 teaspoons sugar

2 cloves garlic, minced

$1^1/_2$ teaspoons Dijon mustard

$1/_2$ teaspoon salt

Pinch of freshly ground black pepper

Makes about $3/_4$ cup

Combine all the ingredients in a small bowl and whisk well. Pour into a cruet or screw-top jar. Shake again before dressing a salad.

# Basic Vinaigrette with Pomegranate Syrup

*Feel free to experiment with other ingredients, such as raspberry vinegar, walnut oil, Dijon mustard, or honey, or just add pomegranate syrup to your favorite dressing.*

---

1/4 cup extra-virgin olive oil

1/4 cup canola oil

2 tablespoons balsamic vinegar

2 tablespoons Pomegranate Syrup (page 15)

2 cloves garlic, minced

Makes about 3/4 cup

Combine all the ingredients in a small bowl and whisk well. Pour into a cruet or screw-top jar. Shake again before dressing a salad.

# Mixed Berry and Pomegranate Coulis

---

1/2 cup pomegranate juice

1/2 cup dry red wine, such as cabernet sauvignon

3 tablespoons sugar

1 (1-inch-long) cinnamon stick

2 tablespoons crème de cassis

1 tablespoon freshly squeezed lemon juice

2 teaspoons vanilla extract

12 ounces (3 cups) frozen mixed berries

Makes 2 1/2 cups

Combine the pomegranate juice, wine, sugar, and cinnamon stick in a small saucepan.

Bring to a boil over high heat, then decrease the heat to a simmer and cook until the liquid is reduced by half.

Add the crème de cassis, lemon juice, vanilla, and frozen berries. Cook just until the berries are thawed and then remove from the heat.

If not using immediately, let cool, cover, and refrigerate until ready to use. The coulis can be reheated or served cold.

# Starters & Soups

Pomegranate Marinated Olives

Drunken Figs with Roquefort in Pomegranate Syrup

Haloumi, Tapenade, and Pomegranate Bites

Antipasti in Pomegranate-Balsamic Dressing

Mango, Pepper, and Pomegranate Salsa

Kumquat, Cranberry, and Pomegranate Relish

Pomegranate Guacamole

Red Pepper, Walnut, and Pomegranate Dip

Bruschetta with Goat Cheese, Red Onion,
and Pomegranate Salsa

Salmon Gravlax with Pomegranate Balsamic Dressing

Stuffed Grape Leaves in Tomato Pomegranate Sauce

Beet and Pomegranate Borscht

Herb and Pomegranate Soup

Yogurt Soup with Pomegranates and Mint

Chilled Melon and Mint Soup with Pomegranates
and Toasted Almonds

# Pomegranate Marinated Olives

*In traditional Jewish-Syrian cuisine, pomegranate marinated olives may be among the delicacies served at a morning buffet to celebrate a special occasion. The sweetness of pomegranate syrup balances the bitterness of the olives. Use only the very best cracked Syrian olives for this dish.*

---

2 cups cracked green Syrian olives, halved and pitted

1 small white onion, chopped

$1/3$ cup Pomegranate Syrup (page 15)

2 tablespoons olive oil

1 tablespoon tomato paste

Makes about $1 1/2$ cups

Combine the olives and onion in a bowl.

In another bowl, stir together the pomegranate syrup, olive oil, and tomato paste. Pour over the olive mixture and stir well.

Cover and marinate in the refrigerator at least overnight.

Bring to room temperature before serving.

# Drunken Figs with Roquefort
# in Pomegranate Syrup

*There is nothing that compares to the taste of rich, creamy cheese combined with a luscious fresh fig. Add Marsala and pomegranate syrup and seeds, and you're in for a real treat.*

8 fresh figs

¹/₃ cup cream cheese

¹/₄ cup any combination of Roquefort, Gorgonzola, and goat cheese, at room temperature

1 tablespoon olive oil

1 clove garlic, crushed

¹/₃ cup pomegranate seeds

¹/₂ cup Marsala wine

2 tablespoons Pomegranate Syrup (page 15)

Serves 4

Preheat the broiler.

Cut an X in the top of each fig, slicing halfway down so that the sides open up like petals.

Combine the cheeses, olive oil, and garlic in a mini food processor or a small bowl and mix well. Fold in the pomegranate seeds.

Carefully spoon about 1 tablespoon of the cheese mixture into each fig. Place the stuffed figs in a baking pan.

Stir together the Marsala and pomegranate syrup in a small bowl and drizzle over the tops of the figs.

Place under the broiler for about 2 minutes, or just until the cheese melts.

# Haloumi, Tapenade, and Pomegranate Bites

*The tapenades improve with time—make them in advance and have them on hand.*

Canapés

16 mini toast rounds

8 ounces haloumi cheese (see note)

Olive oil

8 teaspoons Green Olive Tapenade

8 teaspoons Black Olive tapenade

$1/2$ cup pomegranate seeds, for garnish

Black Olive Tapenade

1 cup pitted good-quality black olives

3 cloves garlic

$1/2$ cup fresh basil leaves

$1/2$ cup olive oil

2 tablespoons balsamic vinegar

Pinch of freshly ground black pepper

Green Olive Tapenade

$1/2$ cup pitted green olives

1 tablespoon drained capers

1 clove garlic, minced

$1/2$ cup pine nuts

$1/8$ teaspoon dried basil

$1/8$ teaspoon dried thyme

$1/2$ cup chopped fresh parsley leaves

2 teaspoons olive oil

1 teaspoon freshly squeezed lemon juice

Freshly ground black pepper

Serves 6 to 8

Make each tapenade separately: To make the black olive tapenade, in a food processor with the motor running, combine the ingredients one by one in the order given (the olive oil should be drizzled in slowly). Stop when the mixture resembles a paste. Transfer to a bowl, cover, and refrigerate. Repeat to make the green olive tapenade.

Arrange the toast rounds on a serving platter and spread each toast with 1 teaspoon of tapenade, alternating between black and green. (Reserve the remaining tapenade for another use.)

Cut the haloumi into 16 slices slightly smaller than the toast rounds. In a skillet, pour in olive oil to a depth of $1/2$ inch and heat over medium-high heat. Fry the cheese slices, turning once, for 1 to 2 minutes on each side, or until golden. Transfer the cheese to paper towels to drain and then place on the toasts. Top with a few pomegranate seeds.

*Note: Haloumi, a semisoft white cheese with an elastic texture, is popular in Cypriot, Greek, and Lebanese cuisine and can be found at ethnic food markets. If unavailable, substitute goat cheese.*

# Antipasti in Pomegranate-Balsamic Dressing

*Who can resist roasted vegetables? They're beautiful, healthful, and versatile as an appetizer, as a side dish, or as part of a Mediterranean buffet, especially when drizzled with pomegranate syrup and balsamic vinegar. Use this vegetable combination as a suggestion and add some of your own favorites.*

---

$1/4$ cup olive oil

2 tablespoons freshly squeezed lemon juice

1 red onion, unpeeled, quartered

1 large bulb fennel, white part only, quartered

1 sweet potato, unpeeled, thickly sliced

3 carrots, peeled and cut into 3-inch lengths

6 cloves garlic, unpeeled

Coarse salt and freshly ground black pepper

Pinch of dried oregano

2 tablespoons Pomegranate Syrup (page 15)

1 tablespoon balsamic vinegar

Serves 4

Preheat the oven to 450°F.

Whisk together the olive oil and lemon juice in a large bowl. Add the onion, fennel, sweet potato, carrots, and garlic and mix well to coat on all sides.

Transfer the vegetables to a baking sheet and arrange in a single layer. Sprinkle with salt, pepper, and oregano to taste. Roast for 20 to 30 minutes, until the vegetables soften and start to brown. Watch carefully so that they don't burn. If some vegetables are done sooner than others, remove them and continue roasting the remaining vegetables.

Transfer the roasted vegetables to a serving platter.

Remove the onion peel before serving.

Stir together the pomegranate syrup and vinegar in a small bowl and pour over the warm vegetables. Serve immediately.

# Mango, Pepper, and Pomegranate Salsa

*A spoonful of this colorful salsa brightens grilled halibut, swordfish—indeed, almost any fish. You may be tempted to eat it straight out of the bowl; go right ahead!*

1 large mango, peeled and cut into ¹/₂-inch cubes

2 green onions, white and green parts, chopped

¹/₂ red onion, thinly sliced

¹/₂ red bell pepper, thinly sliced

¹/₂ yellow bell pepper, thinly sliced

¹/₃ jalapeño chile, seeded and chopped

¹/₄ cup pomegranate seeds

1 tablespoon chopped fresh cilantro leaves

2 tablespoons freshly squeezed orange juice

2 tablespoons olive oil

Serves 4

Combine the mango, green onions, red onion, bell peppers, chile, pomegranate seeds, and cilantro in a bowl.

Whisk together the orange juice and olive oil in a small bowl and pour over the mango mixture.

Cover and refrigerate until ready to use.

# Kumquat, Cranberry, and Pomegranate Relish

*Kumquats add the exotic, cranberries the familiar, and pomegranates the surprise ending! Try it with the Stuffed Cornish Hen with Orange Pomegranate Glaze (page 70), or serve it as a Thanksgiving relish or with a good Stilton or sharp Cheddar on the cheese board.*

3 cups kumquats

$^1/_2$ cup water

$^1/_2$ cup pomegranate juice

1 $^1/_4$ cups sugar

1 tablespoon peeled and grated fresh ginger

$^1/_2$ teaspoon salt

1 pound fresh or frozen cranberries

$^1/_2$ cup golden raisins

$^1/_4$ cup pomegranate seeds

Makes 2 cups

Slice or quarter the kumquats and remove the pits. Combine the kumquats, water, pomegranate juice, sugar, ginger, and salt in a saucepan over medium heat and bring to a boil. Decrease the heat to low and simmer for 5 minutes.

Add the cranberries, increase the heat, and bring to a boil again. Decrease the heat and continue simmering. Once the cranberries burst, scoop out three-quarters of the mixture and set aside.

Continue simmering the remaining mixture until it is reduced by half. Add the raisins and the reserved mixture to the reduction and continue cooking a bit longer.

The entire cooking process should take 30 to 60 minutes—the longer it cooks, the further it reduces and the thicker it gets.

Remove from the heat, let cool, and then fold in the pomegranate seeds. Cover and refrigerate to chill. The relish will keep for one month in the refrigerator.

# Pomegranate Guacamole

*Guacamole studded with pomegranate seeds makes a perfect appetizer to serve with lots of tortilla chips. Better yet, present it at a Mediterranean buffet along with Red Pepper, Walnut, and Pomegranate Dip (opposite page) and Pomegranate Tabbouleh (page 62), accompanied by plenty of toasted pita wedges and fresh vegetables.*

---

2 ripe avocados, peeled and pitted, 1 pit reserved

3 green onions, white and green parts, thinly sliced

1 tablespoon chopped fresh cilantro leaves

1 tablespoon freshly squeezed lemon juice

$1/2$ teaspoon salt

Pinch of white pepper

$1/3$ cup pomegranate seeds

Makes 2 cups

Mash the avocados in a bowl, leaving them a bit chunky.

Mix in the green onions, cilantro, lemon juice, salt, and white pepper. Gently fold in the pomegranate seeds.

Transfer the guacamole to a serving bowl.

If not serving immediately, put the reserved avocado pit into the bowl of guacamole, cover with plastic wrap, and refrigerate. (Adding the pit will prevent the guacamole from turning brown.) Remove the pit before serving.

# Red Pepper, Walnut, and Pomegranate Dip

*Istanbul's Grand Bazaar has been declared a Turkish national treasure, but such honor should also go to this classic dip, known in Turkey as Muhammara. The authentic recipe includes bread, but I think it's perfect without.*

---

2 cups toasted walnuts (see note)

2 cups red bell pepper strips

¹/₂ cup olive oil

2 tablespoons Pomegranate Syrup (page 15)

1 tablespoon ketchup

¹/₂ teaspoon freshly squeezed lemon juice

2 cloves garlic, minced

1 teaspoon ground cumin

¹/₂ teaspoon red pepper flakes

¹/₂ teaspoon salt

Makes 2 cups

Preheat the broiler to roast the bell peppers. Arrange the bell peppers on a greased baking tray and place under the broiler for about 15 minutes, turning the peppers to expose all sides to the heat, until the skins start to blacken and blister. Transfer the roasted peppers to a paper or plastic bag, close, and let stand for 15 to 30 minutes. The peppers will sweat, making it very easy to peel off the skins. Peel and stem the peppers, and cut them into strips; discard the seeds and skins. Keep any juices for marinating: In a bowl, stir together the reserved juices with olive oil, red wine vinegar, and crushed garlic. Add the bell pepper strips, cover, and refrigerate. Drain before using.

Combine all the ingredients in a food processor fitted with the steel blade. Purée until the mixture turns into a brick-colored paste that is slightly grainy. Taste and adjust the seasoning, but keep in mind that the flavor will improve with time.

Transfer the dip to a bowl, cover, and refrigerate until ready to serve. It will keep for 1 week in the refrigerator.

*Note: To toast nuts, place them in a dry skillet over medium-high heat or on a baking tray in a toaster oven. Toast just until they start to turn brown and emit a pleasant aroma. Do not let them burn.*

# Bruschetta with Goat Cheese, Red Onion, and Pomegranate Salsa

*It's fresh, healthful, and delicious. Consider substituting thin baguette slices for the sourdough and serve as canapés.*

---

6 slices sourdough bread

3 tablespoons olive oil

6 tablespoons goat cheese

$1/2$ cup pomegranate seeds

$1/2$ red onion, thinly sliced

$1/2$ jalapeño chile, seeded and finely chopped

1 tablespoon chopped fresh flat-leaf parsley leaves

1 tablespoon chopped fresh basil leaves

Grated zest of 1 lemon

1 tablespoon freshly squeezed lemon juice

Salt and freshly ground black pepper

Serves 3 or 4

Preheat the broiler.

Brush the bread slices on both sides with 2 tablespoons of the olive oil. Arrange the bread on a baking tray and place under the broiler. Toast, turning once, until both sides are golden.

Remove from the broiler and spread 1 tablespoon of the goat cheese on each toast.

Combine the remaining 1 tablespoon of olive oil with the pomegranate seeds, onion, chile, parsley, basil, and lemon zest and juice. Season to taste with salt and pepper and toss gently.

Spoon the mixture on top of the toasts.

# Salmon Gravlax with Pomegranate Balsamic Dressing

*So easy to make, pretty to look at, and delicious to eat.*
*Serve it with a dill mustard sauce and thick slices of country bread.*

---

1 pound fresh salmon fillet, in paper-thin slices

$^1/_2$ cup olive oil

2 tablespoons balsamic vinegar

2 tablespoons Pomegranate Syrup (page 15)

2 tablespoons freshly squeezed lemon juice

Salt and freshly ground black pepper

$^1/_2$ cup fresh basil leaves, chopped

Coarse sea salt

Chopped zest of lemon

$^1/_2$ cup pomegranate seeds

Serves 4

Arrange the salmon slices on a serving dish. Whisk together the olive oil, vinegar, pomegranate syrup, and lemon juice in a bowl. Season to taste with salt and pepper. Pour over the salmon, cover with plastic wrap, and refrigerate for at least 15 minutes.

Just before serving, sprinkle the salmon with the basil, coarse sea salt to taste, lemon zest, and pomegranate seeds.

# Stuffed Grape Leaves in Tomato Pomegranate Sauce

*No ordinary stuffed grape leaves these. The pomegranate syrup adds sweet balance to the tanginess of the grape leaves, making them the ultimate Middle Eastern appetizer. Serve at room temperature with lemon wedges and a bowl of yogurt garnished with fresh mint leaves.*

---

## Grape Leaves

2 tablespoons olive oil

2 small yellow onions, finely chopped

1 cup Basmati or long-grain white rice, rinsed well and drained

2 tablespoons chopped fresh mint leaves

1 teaspoon tomato paste

1 teaspoon Baharat spice (see note)

1 teaspoon chicken soup powder, or 1 chicken bouillon cube

1 teaspoon salt

$^1/_2$ teaspoon freshly ground black pepper

1 (16-ounce) jar preserved grape leaves

$^1/_4$ cup canola oil

1 Russet potato, peeled and thinly sliced

To make the grape leaves, heat the olive oil in a skillet over medium-high heat. Add the onions and sauté for 5 minutes, or until golden. Add the rice and sauté for 2 minutes.

Transfer the rice mixture to a bowl and add the mint leaves, tomato paste, Baharat spice, chicken soup powder, salt, and pepper. Work the mixture with your hands until well combined.

Remove the grape leaves from the jar and squeeze out the excess water.

Working with one leaf at a time, spread the leaf out on a clean surface so that the side with the veins popping up is facing up and the leaf tip is pointing away from you.

Place 1 tablespoon of the rice mixture near the stem end of the leaf. Start to roll up from the bottom and stop one third of the way. Fold in the two sides and continue rolling up from the bottom.

Repeat with all the leaves until you have used up the rice mixture.

Pour the canola oil into the bottom of a large, heavy pot and cover the entire surface with the potato slices (this will prevent the grape leaves from sticking).

Sauce

1 1/2 cups water

4 teaspoons freshly squeezed lemon juice

1 tablespoon Pomegranate Syrup (page 15)

1 tablespoon tomato paste

2 tablespoons sugar

Salt and freshly ground black pepper

Makes about 24 pieces

Start placing a layer of stuffed grape leaves in the pot, seam side down, one next to another, packing them in tightly like sardines. When you have covered the bottom of the pot, start a second layer. Cover the pot, set over low heat, and cook for 10 minutes, giving the leaves a chance to "sweat."

To make the sauce, whisk together the water, lemon juice, pomegranate syrup, tomato paste, and sugar in a bowl. Season to taste with salt and pepper and pour over the grape leaves.

Select a heavy heatproof plate slightly smaller than the diameter of the pot. Invert the plate and place it on top of the leaves (this weighs them down and prevents them from popping up or breaking apart). Bring the liquid to a boil over medium-high heat, decrease the heat to low, cover, and cook for 1 to 1 1/2 hours. The stuffed grape leaves are done when most of the liquid is absorbed and the rice is fully cooked. Allow to cool before serving.

> **Note:** Baharat is a mixture of spices commonly used in Middle Eastern food. To make it yourself, combine equal parts of ground cinnamon, nutmeg, and allspice.

# Beet and Pomegranate Borscht

*Forget all previous associations with borscht. We've left the Russian/Eastern European version in the dust with this upgraded model. Chunks of meat add heartiness further enriched with greens and sweetened with a touch of pomegranate syrup. For a nouvelle version, try straining the borscht and serving as a broth with only chunks of meat and beets. It's a vision in vermillion.*

3 tablespoons canola oil

3 yellow onions, chopped

3 cloves garlic, chopped

1 pound stewing beef, cut into chunks

3 beets, peeled and diced

8 cups water

1/4 cup dried yellow or green split peas, rinsed

3 tablespoons Basmati or long-grain white rice, rinsed

1 cup chopped green onions, white and green parts

1 cup minced fresh flat-leaf parsley leaves

1 cup minced fresh cilantro leaves

2 cups chopped spinach

Salt and freshly ground black pepper

2 tablespoons Pomegranate Syrup (page 15)

Serves 8

Heat the canola oil in a large, heavy pot over medium-high heat. Add the onions and garlic and sauté for 3 to 5 minutes, or until translucent. Add the meat and beets and sauté for 3 minutes. Add 2 cups of the water and bring to a boil. Decrease the heat to low and simmer, covered, for about 1 hour, or until the meat and beets are cooked through. The beets should be fork-tender. Using a slotted spoon, transfer the meat and beets to a plate, cover, and set aside.

Add the remaining 6 cups of water, the split peas, rice, green onions, parsley, cilantro, and spinach to the pot and bring to a boil over high heat. Decrease the heat to low and simmer, covered, for 45 minutes.

Return the meat and beets to the pot and season to taste with salt and pepper. Stir in the pomegranate syrup and cook for 3 minutes. Taste and adjust the seasoning before serving.

# Herb and Pomegranate Soup

*The Persians include meat in their Ashe-e Anar, but this version is vegetarian. Last-minute additions of mint and sautéed onion enhance the sweet and sour flavors.*

4 tablespoons canola oil

1 large yellow onion, chopped, plus 1/2 yellow onion, thinly sliced

3 leeks, white and green parts, chopped

6 celery stalks, including leaves, chopped

2 tablespoons Basmati rice, rinsed

Salt and freshly ground black pepper

6 cups chicken stock, or 6 chicken bouillon cubes dissolved in 6 cups water

2 cups chopped green onions, white and green parts

2 cups minced fresh cilantro leaves

2 cups minced fresh flat-leaf parsley leaves

1 cup chopped spinach

1/4 cup green lentils

2 turnips, peeled and diced

3 to 5 tablespoons Pomegranate Syrup (page 15)

1 tablespoon dried mint

Serves 6 to 8

Heat 3 tablespoons of the canola oil in a large, heavy pot over medium-high heat. Add the chopped yellow onion and sauté for 3 minutes. Add the leeks and celery and continue sautéing until the vegetables are soft. Add the rice, season with salt and pepper, and sauté for 2 minutes.

Add 2 cups of the stock and bring to a boil. Decrease the heat to low and simmer, covered, for about 15 minutes, or until the rice and celery are fully cooked. Remove from the heat and transfer the soup in batches to a blender or food processor. Purée and return to the pot.

Add the remaining 4 cups of stock, the green onions, cilantro, parsley, spinach, and lentils. Bring to a boil over high heat, then decrease the heat to low and simmer, covered, for 45 minutes. Add the turnips and stir in the pomegranate syrup to taste. Cover and simmer for 20 minutes longer.

Just before serving, heat the remaining 1 tablespoon of canola oil in a heavy skillet over high heat. Add the sliced yellow onion and sauté for 5 minutes, or until thoroughly browned. Add the mint, sauté for 30 seconds, and remove from the heat. Stir the onion and mint into the soup and serve immediately.

# Yogurt Soup with Pomegranates and Mint

*This dish was conceived purely for its visual appeal, but the flavorful combination of mint, pomegranates, and walnuts blends beautifully with the yogurt. It's a refreshing soup—ideal for a light dinner on an Indian summer evening.*

4 cups plain yogurt or yogurt drink (see note)

3 cucumbers, peeled, seeded, and finely chopped

4 cloves garlic, minced

3 tablespoons minced fresh dill

Juice of $1/2$ lemon

Salt

Pinch of white pepper

1 tablespoon chopped fresh mint leaves, for garnish

2 tablespoons pomegranate seeds, for garnish

2 tablespoons crushed walnuts, for garnish

Serves 4 to 6

Combine the yogurt, cucumbers, garlic, dill, lemon juice, salt, and white pepper in a bowl and mix well.

Refrigerate to chill for 4 hours.

To serve, ladle the soup into individual bowls and garnish with the chopped mint, pomegranate seeds, and walnuts.

*Note: If using thick yogurt, thin it by adding 4 ice cubes to the soup before placing in the refrigerator to chill.*

# Chilled Melon and Mint Soup with Pomegranates and Toasted Almonds

*Who says you can't improve on perfection? As a Middle Eastern dessert, melon soup is often paired with almonds or almond milk. A sprinkling of mint leaves and pomegranate seeds adds sweetness and a slightly exotic flair. Consider garnishing with balls of cantaloupe for a spectacularly colorful effect.*

---

$2^{1}/_{2}$ pounds ripe honeydew melon, halved and seeded

$^{1}/_{4}$ cup fresh mint leaves plus additional for garnish

2 tablespoons freshly squeezed lime juice

$^{1}/_{2}$ teaspoon salt

Pinch of sugar (optional)

$^{1}/_{4}$ cup toasted almond slivers, for garnish (see note, page 31)

$^{1}/_{2}$ cup pomegranate seeds, for garnish

Serves 4 to 6

Using a sharp knife, remove the melon rind and cube the melon flesh.

Combine the melon cubes, $^{1}/_{4}$ cup of the mint leaves, the lime juice, and salt in a food processor fitted with the steel blade. Purée until it liquefies. Taste and adjust the seasoning, adding a bit of sugar if the soup is too tart. Refrigerate to chill for 4 hours.

When ready to serve, ladle the soup into individual bowls and garnish with the additional mint leaves, almonds, and pomegranate seeds.

# Salads & Side Dishes

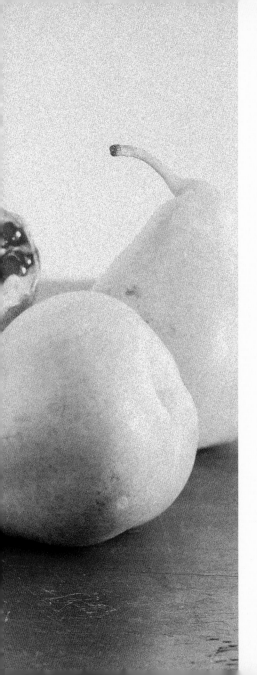

Grilled Pear, Goat Cheese, and Pomegranate Salad

Celebration Salad with Pomegranate Poppy Seed Dressing

Endive, Avocado, and Grapefruit Salad

Curried Chicken Salad with Grapes, Pecans, and Pomegranates

Rice, Seafood, and Pomegranate Salad

Grilled Haloumi, Blue Cheese, and Pomegranate Salad

Rum and Sweet Potato Purée with Pomegranate Pecans

Okra Stew in Tomato Pomegranate Sauce

Parsley Salad with Feta, Almonds, and Pomegranates

Jeweled Rice with Pistachios, Apricots, and Pomegranates

Couscous, Peanut, and Pomegranate Salad

Quinoa Salad with Herbs, Feta, and Pomegranate

Pomegranate Tabbouleh

Wheat Berries with Pecans, Raisins, and Pomegranate

# Grilled Pear, Goat Cheese, and Pomegranate Salad

*The pomegranate-soaked pears add just the right touch of sweetness*
*to complement the bitter greens and creamy goat cheese.*

2 Bosc or Red Bartlett pears, peeled and sliced

2 tablespoons Pomegranate Syrup (page 15)

1 tablespoon unsalted butter

4 to 6 cups mixed arugula and watercress leaves

$^{1}/_{2}$ cup Basic Vinaigrette with Pomegranate Syrup (page 19)

1 goat cheese log, sliced into 12 pieces

$^{1}/_{2}$ cup pomegranate seeds, for garnish

Serves 4

Place the pear slices in a small bowl, drizzle the pomegranate syrup over them, and turn gently to coat well. Let stand for 10 minutes.

Melt the butter in a skillet over medium-high heat. When it starts to sizzle, add the pear slices and sauté just until they start to caramelize. Do not let them get too soft.

Tear the arugula and watercress leaves into bite-size pieces. Arrange the greens on 4 individual plates and drizzle each with a little of the vinaigrette. Slide the pear slices from the skillet onto the greens.

Arrange 3 slices of goat cheese around each plate. Sprinkle with the pomegranate seeds and serve immediately.

# Celebration Salad with Pomegranate Poppy Seed Dressing

*This salad calls for a celebration—it is an absolute spectacle of color that will inspire any party at your table.*

8 cups mixed salad greens

2 heads Belgian endive, trimmed and coarsely chopped

1 red onion, thinly sliced into half rounds

1 avocado, peeled and cubed

2 navel oranges, peeled and cut into bite-size pieces, membranes removed

1 red grapefruit, peeled and cut into bite-size pieces, membranes removed

1 cup black olive rings

1 cup pomegranate seeds

2 tablespoons poppy seeds

1 cup Basic Vinaigrette with Pomegranate Juice (page 18)

Serves 6 to 8

Place the greens and endive in a large serving bowl and add the onion, avocado, orange and grapefruit pieces, olives, and $1/2$ cup of the pomegranate seeds.

Add the poppy seeds to the vinaigrette, shake well, and dress the salad.

Toss gently and sprinkle the remaining pomegranate seeds on top.

# Endive, Avocado, and Grapefruit Salad

*If you have five minutes to spare, you can create the most beautiful salad—so few ingredients for such tasty perfection!*

---

2 heads Belgian endive, trimmed and
  leaves separated

1 avocado, peeled and sliced

1 red grapefruit, peeled and cut into
  sections, membranes removed

$^1/_2$ cup pomegranate seeds

Fresh cilantro leaves, for garnish

2 tablespoons Basic Vinaigrette with
  Pomegranate Syrup (page 19)

Serves 2

Arrange the endive leaves on individual plates and top with the avocado slices and grapefruit pieces.

Sprinkle with the pomegranate seeds and garnish with cilantro.

Drizzle the vinaigrette over the salads.

# Curried Chicken Salad with Grapes, Pecans, and Pomegranates

*Who can resist chicken salad with sweet pomegranate seeds mixed in? Drizzling the bed of lettuce with the vinaigrette enhances the pomegranate presence, but you may prefer to leave the lettuce plain. For an extra kick, add fresh pineapple chunks and a sprinkling of coconut.*

---

3 cups chicken stock, or 3 chicken bouillon cubes dissolved in 3 cups water

1 pound chicken breasts, boned and skinned

²/₃ cup seedless red or green grapes, halved

²/₃ cup pecans, broken into quarters

2 tablespoons mayonnaise

¹/₂ teaspoon curry powder

Salt and freshly ground black pepper

¹/₂ cup pomegranate seeds plus additional for garnish

Red-leaf and green-leaf lettuce leaves

3 tablespoons Basic Vinaigrette with Pomegranate Syrup (page 19)

Serves 2 or 3

In a saucepan, bring the chicken stock to a boil. Add the chicken breasts, decrease the heat to a simmer, and poach for 6 minutes, or until done. Test for doneness by slicing into the thickest part of the breast.

Transfer the chicken to a plate and discard the poaching liquid. Let the chicken breasts cool and then cut them into 1-inch cubes.

Combine the grapes, pecans, mayonnaise, and curry powder in a bowl. Mix well and season to taste with salt and pepper. Add the chicken and mix well.

Sprinkle in ¹/₂ cup of the pomegranate seeds, cover with plastic wrap, and refrigerate to chill.

When ready to serve, prepare a bed of lettuce leaves on a serving platter or individual plates. Drizzle the leaves with the vinaigrette and then top with a mound of chicken salad.

Garnish with additional pomegranate seeds.

# Rice, Seafood, and Pomegranate Salad

*Including pomegranate seeds in this delicious salad adds
another dimension of flavor and color.*

1 cup white and wild rice mix or Basmati rice

$^1/_2$ red onion, thinly sliced

4 green onions, white part only, chopped

$^1/_4$ cup finely chopped fresh flat-leaf parsley
leaves

$^1/_4$ cup finely chopped fresh cilantro leaves

2 tablespoons finely chopped fresh mint leaves

$^1/_4$ cup olive oil

Juice of 1 lemon

Salt and freshly ground black pepper

1 pound poached mixed seafood (such as
shrimp, mussels, and calamari)

$^1/_2$ cup pomegranate seeds plus additional for
garnish

Serves 4 to 6

Prepare the white and wild rice mix according to package directions. (If using Basmati, cook the rice as instructed on page 58.) Allow it to cool.

In a large bowl, combine the red onion, green onions, parsley, cilantro, and mint. Drizzle with the olive oil and lemon juice. Season to taste with salt and pepper.

Add the cooled rice and toss to mix well. Fold in the seafood and $^1/_2$ cup of the pomegranate seeds.

Cover and refrigerate.

When ready to serve, transfer to a serving bowl and garnish with additional pomegranate seeds.

Serve cold or at room temperature.

# Grilled Haloumi, Blue Cheese, and Pomegranate Salad

*As if giving us Aphrodite were not enough, the island of Cyprus has also bestowed upon us haloumi cheese! This delicacy is fried briefly and served with salad, as in this recipe, or on crackers for an appetizer, garnished with fresh mint, black cumin seeds, or lemon wedges. Yum!*

---

3 cups mixed baby greens

1 Bosc or Red Bartlett pear, peeled and sliced

1 cucumber, peeled and diced

1/2 avocado, peeled and sliced

8 cherry tomatoes, halved

2 ounces blue cheese, crumbled

1/3 cup pomegranate seeds

4 ounces haloumi cheese or semisoft goat cheese (see page 24)

2 tablespoons olive oil

8 baguette slices, toasted

1/4 cup Basic Vinaigrette with Pomegranate Juice (page 18)

Serves 2

Place the greens in a bowl. Add the pear, cucumber, avocado, tomatoes, blue cheese, and half of the pomegranate seeds and toss gently.

Cut the haloumi cheese into 8 slices slightly smaller than the baguette slices. Heat the olive oil in a skillet over medium heat. Fry the slices, turning once, for 1 to 2 minutes on each side, or until golden. Transfer the slices to paper towels to drain and then place on the toasts. (If using goat cheese, preheat the broiler. Place a slice of goat cheese on each baguette slice and broil just until the cheese turns golden.)

Dress the salad with the vinaigrette and toss gently. Divide the salad between 2 individual plates. Sprinkle the remaining pomegranate seeds on top and arrange 4 cheese toasts around each plate.

# Rum and Sweet Potato Purée
# with Pomegranate Pecans

*If nuts are perfect with sweet potatoes, wouldn't the addition of pecans caramelized in pomegranate molasses be heaven? Try it and see if you don't agree.*

---

3 to 4 pounds sweet potatoes, peeled and cut into small chunks

6 tablespoons unsalted butter, at room temperature

2 tablespoons dark rum

1 tablespoon dark brown sugar

1$^{1}/_{2}$ teaspoons salt

1 cup coarsely chopped pecans

3 tablespoons Pomegranate Molasses (page 16)

Serves 6

Preheat the oven to 350°F.

Place the sweet potatoes in a saucepan with water to cover and bring to a boil. Decrease the heat to low, cover, and simmer for 10 to 15 minutes, until tender. Drain and let cool in a colander.

In a food processor fitted with the steel blade, purée the sweet potatoes in batches. Transfer the purée to a large bowl. Stir in the butter, rum, brown sugar, and salt.

Toss the chopped pecans in a dry skillet over medium-high heat for 3 to 5 minutes. Add the pomegranate molasses and cook for 2 to 3 minutes, just until the pecans are well coated and start to caramelize. Remove from the heat, let cool slightly for 2 minutes, then add to the sweet potato mixture.

Transfer the mixture to a shallow baking dish. Bake for about 45 minutes, or until the mixture is set and the edges start to turn brown.

# Okra Stew in Tomato Pomegranate Sauce

*One of the very few foods I always took a pass on was okra, or bamya, as it's known in the Middle East. Until now. Cooking this vegetable with tomato paste and pomegranate syrup makes all the difference. Serve with Basmati rice and lemon wedges to squeeze over it.*

---

3 tablespoons canola oil

1 yellow onion, chopped

1 pound frozen whole okra

2 cloves garlic, chopped

1 tomato, peeled and grated

$1/2$ cup tomato paste diluted in 1 cup warm water

$1/4$ cup Pomegranate Syrup (page 15)

$1/4$ cup freshly squeezed lemon juice

1 tablespoon sugar

$1^1/_2$ cups water

Serves 6

Heat the canola oil in a large skillet over high heat. Add the onion and sauté for 3 to 5 minutes, or until it is translucent.

Add the okra and fry for 3 to 4 minutes, until evenly browned.

Stir in the garlic, grated tomato, diluted tomato paste, pomegranate syrup, lemon juice, and sugar.

Pour in the water and bring to a boil. Decrease the heat to low, cover, and cook for 10 to 15 minutes, until the okra is tender.

# Parsley Salad with Feta, Almonds, and Pomegranates

*If you can imagine eating a bowl of freshness, this has to be it.*
*Serve with almost any main course, or make a meal ofthis salad with*
*a loaf of crusty bread and a bowl of Herb and Pomegranate Soup (page 40).*

---

Salad

3 cups fresh flat-leaf parsley leaves

$^1/_2$ cup almond slivers

2 ounces feta cheese, crumbled

$^3/_4$ cup pomegranate seeds


Dressing

2 tablespoons canola oil

2 tablespoons olive oil

2 tablespoons pomegranate juice

1 tablespoon freshly squeezed lemon juice

1 tablespoon cider vinegar

1 clove garlic, crushed

$^1/_2$ teaspoon salt

$^1/_2$ teaspoon sugar

Pinch of chili powder


Serves 2 or 3

Place the parsley leaves in a serving bowl.

Add the almonds, feta, and pomegranate seeds and toss.

Combine all the dressing ingredients in a cruet or screw-top jar and mix well.

Pour over the parsley salad and toss.

# Jeweled Rice with Pistachios, Apricots, and Pomegranates

*Jeweled Rice is the quintessential Persian pilaf, and no one makes it like my friend Eysar. Eliminating the usual saffron (hard to find) and barberries (impossible to find), I arrived at a delicious alternative—a pomegranate version! It's delightful served with almost any chicken, lamb, or fish main course. (See picture, page 73.)*

2 cups Basmati or long-grain white rice, rinsed several times and cooked (see note)

1/4 cup dried cranberries

1/2 cup chopped dried apricots

1/2 cup toasted pistachio pieces (see note, page 31)

1/2 cup toasted almond slivers (see note, page 31)

1/4 cup pomegranate seeds

Serves 8 to 10

Cover the dried cranberries with warm water and soak for 10 minutes, or until they plump up. Drain the cranberries.

Combine the cranberries, apricots, pistachios, and almonds in a large bowl. Add the warm rice and mix well. Spoon the mixture onto a serving platter, mounding it in the center like a pyramid. Sprinkle the pomegranate seeds on top and serve.

*Note: Combine 2 cups rice, 5 cups chicken stock, and 2 tablespoons olive oil in a saucepan and bring to a boil over medium-high heat. Decrease the heat to low, cover, and cook. After 20 minutes, uncover and check the rice—if the water is not yet absorbed, re-cover and cook until rice is ready. If no water remains and the rice is still hard, add 1/3 cup boiling water to the pan. When the rice is tender, remove from the heat.*

# Couscous, Peanut, and Pomegranate Salad

*Avi Rophe, the Middle Eastern food maven, is the inspiration for this recipe. Avi uses bulghur instead of couscous, but I received his blessing to make the substitution and I think it tastes even better than the original. Try either version and decide for yourself.*

1 cup medium-grain instant couscous

1 chicken bouillon cube dissolved in 1 cup
  boiling water

1/4 cup currants

2 cups fresh flat-leaf parsley leaves, coarsely
  chopped

1 cup fresh cilantro leaves, coarsely chopped

1/2 cucumber, peeled, seeded, and diced

1/2 jalapeño chile, seeded and diced

1/3 cup toasted peanuts or almonds, coarsely
  chopped (see note, page 31)

1/2 cup pomegranate seeds

1/2 teaspoon salt

1/2 cup olive oil

Juice of 1/2 lemon

Serves 4

Put the couscous in a shallow bowl and add the hot bouillon.

Let stand for 5 minutes, or until all the liquid is absorbed, then fluff up the couscous with a fork. (Or make the couscous according to package directions.)

Cover the currants with warm water and let soak while you prepare the remaining ingredients. Drain the currants.

In a serving bowl, combine the couscous, currants, parsley, cilantro, cucumber, chile, nuts, pomegranate seeds, and salt. Mix well.

When ready to serve, whisk together the olive oil and lemon juice in a small bowl and pour over the salad. Serve at room temperature.

# Quinoa Salad with Herbs, Feta, and Pomegranate

*Quinoa, the "newly discovered" darling of the grain world, was actually eaten by the ancient Incas. If only they'd had a line of communication open with the ancient Hebrews—no doubt pomegranates would have been added to the dish!*

---

1 cup quinoa

2 cups chicken stock or water

1 cup baby peas

$^1/_2$ cup crumbled feta cheese

$^1/_2$ red onion, chopped

$^1/_2$ red bell pepper, diced

$^1/_3$ cup mixed chopped fresh basil, flat-leaf parsley, and cilantro leaves

2 tablespoons chopped fresh tarragon leaves

$^1/_2$ cup pomegranate seeds

$^1/_4$ cup pomegranate juice

1 tablespoon orange juice concentrate, thawed

1 tablespoon white wine vinegar

2 teaspoons freshly squeezed lemon juice

1 tablespoon olive oil

Salt and freshly ground black pepper

Serves 4

Spread the quinoa out on a dish and pick out any pieces of grit. Rinse the grains thoroughly in a fine-mesh sieve and drain well.

In a saucepan over high heat, bring the stock to a boil, stir in the quinoa, and return to a boil. Decrease the heat to low, cover, and simmer for about 15 minutes, or until all the liquid is absorbed. The quinoa should be tender but not mushy. Remove from the heat and fluff up the quinoa with a fork. Transfer to a serving bowl and let cool.

While the quinoa is cooking, cook and cool the peas. Place the peas and enough water to cover them in a saucepan. Bring the water to a boil, then decrease the heat to low and simmer for about 5 minutes. Remove from the heat to cool.

Add the cooled peas, feta, onion, bell pepper, mixed herbs, tarragon, and pomegranate seeds to the cooled quinoa. Toss to mix well.

In a small bowl, whisk together the pomegranate juice, orange juice concentrate, vinegar, lemon juice, and olive oil. Season to taste with salt and pepper. Set aside.

Just before serving, whisk the dressing again, pour over the salad, and toss.

# Pomegranate Tabbouleh

*When Linda Zaga, my friend and a Syrian food consultant, told me about growing up in Aleppo and eating tabbouleh flavored with pomegranates, I had my culinary doubts. But lo and behold—this staple of the Middle Eastern buffet is a knockout made with pomegranate syrup and tomato paste.*

---

1 cup fine-grain bulghur

$^3/_4$ cup boiling water

1 medium yellow onion, finely chopped

$^1/_3$ cup Pomegranate Syrup (page 15)

$^1/_2$ cup chopped walnuts

2 tablespoons chopped fresh flat-leaf parsley

$1^1/_2$ tablespoons olive oil

$1^1/_2$ tablespoons tomato paste

$1^1/_2$ teaspoons chile paste or Tabasco

1 teaspoon freshly squeezed lemon juice

1 teaspoon salt

Serves 4 to 6

Spread the bulghur out on a dish and pick out any pieces of grit.

Place in a bowl, add the boiling water, and let stand for about 1 hour, or until all the water is absorbed. Using your hands, squeeze out any excess moisture. The bulghur should become tender but maintain its graininess.

Put the bulghur in a serving bowl and add the onion, pomegranate syrup, walnuts, parsley, olive oil, tomato paste, chile paste, lemon juice, and salt. Mix well, then taste and adjust the seasoning.

Cover and refrigerate. Bring to room temperature before serving.

# Wheat Berries with Pecans, Raisins, and Pomegranate

*The wheat berries provide crunchiness, the cumin and turmeric lend a foreign flair, and the pomegranate juice and seeds add a touch of sweetness.*

2 cups wheat berries

7 cups water

$^1/_2$ cup raisins

$^1/_3$ cup pomegranate juice

1 tablespoon unsalted butter

1 tablespoon olive oil

1 red onion, chopped

2 cloves garlic, minced

1 cup pecans, toasted and chopped (see note, page 31)

$^1/_2$ teaspoon ground cumin

$^1/_2$ teaspoon ground turmeric

$^1/_2$ teaspoon chile powder

1 teaspoon salt

Freshly ground black pepper

$^1/_2$ cup pomegranate seeds, for garnish

Serves 6 to 8

Spread the wheat berries out on a dish and pick out any pieces of grit. Rinse them several times in a sieve and drain well.

Bring the water to a boil in a large saucepan and add the wheat berries. Decrease the heat to medium-low and cook, uncovered, for about 45 minutes, or until the berries are tender. They should still be firm, not too tough or too soft. Remove from the heat and drain.

Soak the raisins in the pomegranate juice for 15 minutes, or until they plump up. Drain the raisins, reserving the juice.

Melt the butter with the olive oil in a large skillet over medium heat. Add the onion and sauté for 3 to 5 minutes, or until translucent. Add the garlic, sauté for 1 minute, and then stir in the pecans, spices, salt, and pepper to taste. Add the wheat berries in batches, stirring between additions. Add the raisins and a bit of the reserved soaking juice (add all of the juice if the mixture seems dry). Taste and adjust the seasoning. Transfer to a serving dish and garnish with the pomegranate seeds.

# Main Courses

Walnut, Date, and Pomegranate Chicken

Bacon-Wrapped Chicken Roll-ups with Goat Cheese
in Pomegranate Cream Sauce

Chicken in Root Vegetable, Pomegranate and Dried Fruit Sauce

Stuffed Cornish Hen with Orange Pomegranate Glaze

Duck Breasts in Apricot, Shallot, and Pomegranate Sauce

Stuffed Squash in Tomato-Pomegranate Sauce

Spareribs in Pomegranate Barbecue Sauce

Meat, Pine Nut, and Pomegranate Pastries

Veal Scaloppine in Port and Pomegranate Sauce

Lamb Stew with Dried Fruit, Chestnuts, and Pomegranate Syrup

Grilled Beef Fillet with Caramelized Shallot, Marsala,
and Pomegranate Marmalade

Seared Salmon Fillets with Pomegranate Sherry Glaze

Tuna, Asparagus, and Pomegranate Stir-Fry

Shrimp in Brandy and Pomegranate Cream Sauce

# Walnut, Date, and Pomegranate Chicken

*Anyone knowledgeable about classic Persian cuisine will recognize a variation of*
*Khoresh-e Fesenjan, chicken with walnuts and pomegranates.*
*This version is minus the usual saffron and squash but with a wonderful addition*
*of dates. After two hours of cooking, the chicken will melt in your mouth.*

---

3 tablespoons canola oil

2 yellow onions, sliced

2 pounds (about 20) chicken drumsticks, skinned

$1/_2$ cup Pomegranate Syrup (page 15) diluted in $1^1/_2$ cups water

1 tablespoon sugar

1 teaspoon salt

2 cups toasted walnuts, finely ground (see note, page 31)

$3/_4$ cup chopped and pitted dates

Pomegranate seeds, for garnish

Serves 8

Heat the canola oil in a Dutch oven or large pot over medium-high heat. Add the onions and sauté for 3 to 5 minutes, or until translucent. Add the drumsticks and sauté until browned.

Stir in the diluted pomegranate syrup, sugar, and salt. Add the walnuts and dates and stir gently.

Bring to a boil, decrease the heat to low, cover, and simmer for about 2 hours. Check and stir occasionally. Add water if the stew is too thick.

Cook until the chicken is extremely soft and the dates have melted into the stew.

Garnish with pomegranate seeds before serving.

# Bacon-Wrapped Chicken Roll-ups with Goat Cheese in Pomegranate Cream Sauce

*Dare to take a bit of culinary license with coq au vin—and this dish is the inspired result.*

6 chicken breasts, boned and skinned

$^1/_3$ cup Pomegranate Syrup (page 15) plus additional for brushing

24 fresh sage leaves

1 goat cheese log, sliced into 12 pieces

$^2/_3$ cup pomegranate seeds

12 slices bacon

1 tablespoon unsalted butter

$^1/_4$ cup olive oil

3 cloves garlic, chopped

1 tablespoon Worcestershire sauce

$^1/_4$ cup semi-dry white wine

$^1/_3$ cup whipping cream

Salt and freshly ground black pepper

Serves 6

Cut each chicken breast in half lengthwise. Pound the chicken pieces to flatten them. Brush each piece with pomegranate syrup. Place 2 sage leaves, 1 slice of goat cheese, and about 1 teaspoon of pomegranate seeds on top of each chicken piece. Roll up, place the chicken roll on a slice of bacon, and roll up again, completely covering the chicken with the bacon.

Melt the butter with the olive oil in a skillet over medium heat. Place the bacon-wrapped chicken rolls seam side down in the skillet. Cover the pan and fry, turning occasionally, for 5 minutes. Uncover and stir in the garlic, Worcestershire sauce, $^1/_3$ cup of the pomegranate syrup, and wine. Stir in the cream, season to taste with salt and pepper, and remove from the heat.

Arrange 2 roll-ups on each individual plate and drizzle the sauce on and around the roll-ups. Serve immediately.

# Chicken in Root Vegetable, Pomegranate and Dried Fruit Sauce

*Ah, the aroma that fills the house when this is cooking. Serve accompanied with Rum and Sweet Potato Purée (page 54) or baby potatoes roasted with garlic and rosemary.*

---

1/4 cup Pomegranate Syrup (page 15)

2 tablespoons olive oil

2 tablespoons HP brand brown sauce

6 cloves garlic, crushed

1/2 teaspoon red pepper flakes

6 chicken thighs

6 chicken drumsticks

Sauce

2 tablespoons olive oil

4 cloves garlic, crushed

1 yellow onion, chopped

6 shallots, peeled

1 carrot, peeled and cubed

1 celery root, peeled and cubed

3/4 cup dried apricots

1/2 cup golden raisins

Salt and freshly ground black pepper

1/2 cup water

Grated zest of 1 lemon

1/3 cup Pomegranate Syrup (page 15)

2 tablespoons chopped fresh basil leaves

1 teaspoon chopped fresh thyme leaves

1/4 cup chopped fresh flat-leaf parsley leaves, for garnish

1/2 cup pomegranate seeds, for garnish

Serves 6 to 8

Preheat the oven to 400°F.

Combine the pomegranate syrup, olive oil, brown sauce, garlic, and red pepper flakes in a large bowl. Drench the chicken pieces in the mixture, turning until well coated. Transfer the chicken to a roasting pan and bake for 30 minutes. Decrease the temperature to 350°F and bake for 10 minutes longer.

To make the sauce, heat the olive oil in a skillet over medium heat. Add the garlic, onion, shallots, carrot, and celery root and sauté for 8 to 10 minutes, or until the mixture starts to brown. Stir in the apricots and raisins, season to taste with salt and black pepper, and cook for 5 minutes longer. Add the water, lemon zest, pomegranate syrup, basil, and thyme. Stir while bringing to a boil, then decrease the heat to low and cook for 30 minutes longer, or until all the vegetables have softened.

Arrange the baked chicken pieces on a serving platter. Pour the sauce over the chicken and sprinkle with the parsley and pomegranate seeds.

# Stuffed Cornish Hen with Orange Pomegranate Glaze

*Serve this elegant dish with the Kumquat, Cranberry, and Pomegranate Relish (page 28) and a side of steamed vegetables, such as asparagus or green beans.*

Stuffing

2 tablespoons olive oil

1 medium yellow onion, chopped

$1/4$ cup long-grain white rice, rinsed

$1/3$ cup water

5 ounces chicken livers, cleaned

2 tablespoons Pomegranate Syrup (page 15)

1 tablespoon brandy

$1/2$ cup chopped walnuts

1 tablespoon chopped fresh thyme leaves, or 1 teaspoon dried thyme

3 tablespoons chopped fresh flat-leaf parsley leaves

3 tablespoons pomegranate seeds

$1/2$ teaspoon Baharat spice (see note, page 36)

Salt and freshly ground black pepper

Preheat the oven to 450°F.

To make the stuffing, heat the olive oil in a skillet over high heat. Add the onion and sauté for 5 minutes, or until browned. Stir in the rice, then add the water, and cook until the water is absorbed (rice must be slightly cooked when used as stuffing).

Finely chop the livers and transfer to a bowl. Stir in the pomegranate syrup and brandy. Add the rice mixture, walnuts, thyme, parsley, pomegranate seeds, and Baharat spice. Season with salt and pepper. Mix well and set aside.

Wash the Cornish hen and pat dry. Combine the olive oil and pomegranate syrup in a bowl and season to taste with salt and pepper. Rub the hen inside and out with the oil mixture.

Place the hen in an oiled roasting pan. Stuff the cavity three-fourths full with the liver stuffing. Spoon some stuffing between the breast skin and the flesh. Put any remaining stuffing in the pan around the hen. Close the opening with skewers and tie the drumsticks together with string.

Marinade

1 (2-pound) Cornish hen

2 tablespoons olive oil

1 tablespoon Pomegranate Syrup (page 15)

Salt and freshly ground black pepper

Glaze

$^1/_2$ cup freshly squeezed orange juice

$^1/_2$ cup pomegranate juice

2 fresh sage leaves

1 tablespoon balsamic vinegar

Freshly ground black pepper


Chopped fresh flat-leaf parsley leaves, for
    garnish

Pomegranate seeds, for garnish


Serves 2

Cover the pan with aluminum foil (or use a covered roasting pan). Roast the hen for 30 minutes, then uncover and roast for 15 to 30 minutes longer, or until cooked through.

To make the glaze, combine the orange juice and pomegranate juice in a saucepan over high heat and cook until the liquid is reduced by half. Remove from the heat and stir in the sage leaves, vinegar, and pepper to taste.

Transfer the roasted hen to a serving platter. Pour the glaze over it and garnish with parsley and pomegranate seeds.

# Duck Breasts in Apricot, Shallot, and Pomegranate Sauce

*This succulent dish is perfect paired with the Jeweled Rice with Pistachios, Apricots, and Pomegranates (page 58).*

Sauce

2 tablespoons olive oil

4 shallots, peeled

3 cloves garlic, chopped

2 tablespoons honey

$1/_2$ cup pomegranate juice

$1/_2$ cup chicken stock

$1/_3$ cup Riesling or semi-dry white wine

$1/_3$ cup dried apricots, chopped

2 tablespoons chopped fresh parsley leaves

1 tablespoon chopped fresh thyme leaves,
    or $1/_2$ teaspoon dried thyme

Salt and freshly ground black pepper

$1/_2$ cup pomegranate seeds


4 duck breasts, boned

2 tablespoons olive oil

Salt and freshly ground black pepper

Pomegranate seeds, for garnish


Serves 4

To make the sauce, heat the olive oil in a skillet over medium-high heat. Add the shallots and garlic and sauté for 2 minutes. Stir in the honey, followed by the pomegranate juice, stock, and wine. Continue stirring while adding the apricots, parsley, thyme, and salt and pepper to taste. Bring to a boil, decrease the heat to low, and simmer until the liquid is reduced and thickened to a sauce, about 15 minutes. Stir in the pomegranate seeds and remove from the heat.

Prick the skin of the duck breasts in several places and rub with the olive oil. Season with salt and pepper. Heat a large, heavy skillet over medium heat. Place the duck breasts skin side down in the skillet. Cook for 15 to 20 minutes, until most of the fat has burned off and the meat is almost cooked through. Turn the breasts over and cook the other side for about 3 minutes, or until the meat is medium-rare. It should appear brown around the edges and pink inside.

Transfer the duck breasts skin side down to a cutting board. Let rest for 10 minutes and then cut on the diagonal into thin slices. Fan the slices out on individual plates. Drizzle the sauce over and garnish with pomegranate seeds.

# Stuffed Squash in Tomato-Pomegranate Sauce

*Stuffed vegetables are a staple of Mediterranean cuisine. If you can cut it and core it,*
*you can stuff it! The tomato paste, lemon juice, and pomegranate syrup sauce*
*adds a sweet-and-sour twist to the dish.*

Stuffed Squash

8 medium globe zucchini

$1/2$ pound ground beef

1 cup short-grain white rice, rinsed

1 yellow onion, chopped

1 tomato, peeled and grated

$3/4$ cup olive oil

1 tablespoon Pomegranate Syrup (page 15)

$1/2$ cup pine nuts

1 teaspoon Baharat spice (see note, page 36)

Salt and freshly ground black pepper

Sauce

2 cups water

$1/4$ cup tomato paste

$1/2$ cup freshly squeezed lemon juice

3 tablespoons Pomegranate Syrup (page 15)

1 tablespoon sugar

Salt and freshly ground black pepper

Serves 8

Slice off the tops of the squash and reserve. Scoop out the flesh and chop half of it (discard the other half or reserve for another use). Transfer the chopped flesh to a bowl and add the beef, rice, onion, tomato, $1/4$ cup of the olive oil, pomegranate syrup, pine nuts, and Baharat spice. Season with salt and pepper. Use your hands to mix the ingredients together.

Fill each squash two-thirds full with the rice mixture (leaving room for the rice to expand). Cover with the tops of the squash and place in a wide, deep saucepan. Pour the remaining $1/2$ cup of olive oil around the squash, cover, and cook over low heat for 5 minutes (just to give the squash a head start before the sauce is added).

To make the sauce, whisk together the water, tomato paste, lemon juice, pomegranate syrup, and sugar in a bowl. Season with salt and pepper to taste. Pour the sauce over the squash in the pan. Increase the heat to medium-high and bring the sauce to a boil. Decrease the heat to low, cover, and simmer for 1 to $1 1/2$ hours, until the beef and rice are thoroughly cooked. Serve hot.

# Spareribs in Pomegranate Barbecue Sauce

*Who can resist spareribs? If you're one of the few, use this sauce recipe for any meat or chicken dish that calls for a barbecue sauce. Serve with Antipasti in Pomegranate-Balsamic Dressing (page 26) and a chilled bottle of cabernet blanc.*

Barbecue Sauce

4 cloves garlic, crushed

$^1/_3$ cup Pomegranate Syrup (page 15)

$^1/_4$ cup olive oil

1 tablespoon balsamic vinegar

1 teaspoon Worcestershire sauce

1 teaspoon teriyaki sauce

$^1/_2$ teaspoon chile paste

Salt and freshly ground black pepper

16 spareribs

Serves 4

Preheat the oven to 500°F.

To make the barbecue sauce, combine the garlic, pomegranate syrup, olive oil, vinegar, Worcestershire sauce, teriyaki sauce, and chile paste in a bowl. Stir well and season to taste with salt and pepper.

Coat the spareribs by either rubbing or brushing them with the sauce.

Place the spareribs in a roasting pan, one next to another, without overlapping them.

Roast for 20 minutes, turning once after 10 minutes so that both sides get evenly done.

# Meat, Pine Nut, and Pomegranate Pastries

*In the Middle East, these popular pizza-style meat pastries are known as Lahm B'Ajeen,*
*literally "meat and dough." They can be made with beef or lamb atop rounds of yeast dough,*
*phyllo, or ready-made pita, and served with lemon wedges and yogurt alongside.*

---

Dough

3 cups all-purpose flour

2 teaspoons salt

1 teaspoon fast-rising active dry yeast

1 tablespoon olive oil

1 to 1¹/₄ cups warm water


Topping

1 pound ground beef

1 large yellow onion, chopped

¹/₂ cup Pomegranate Syrup (page 15)

1 tablespoon chile paste

1 tablespoon tomato paste

¹/₂ teaspoon salt

1 teaspoon Baharat spice (see note, page 36)

Freshly ground black pepper


¹/₂ cup pine nuts

¹/₂ cup pomegranate seeds

Makes about 12 pastries

To make the dough, combine the flour, salt, and yeast in a food processor fitted with the steel blade. With the motor running, slowly drizzle in the olive oil through the feed tube. Drizzle in just enough water so that the dough forms a ball and is slightly sticky to the touch. (You can also make the dough by hand or with an electric mixer following the same steps for preparing it in a food processor.) Transfer the ball of dough to an oiled bowl, cover with a kitchen towel, and let rise for 1 to 2 hours, or until doubled in size.

Preheat the oven to 400°F. Lightly oil two baking sheets.

To make the topping, in a bowl combine the beef, onion, pomegranate syrup, chile paste, tomato paste, salt, Baharat spice, and pepper to taste. Mix well (working it with your hands and squeezing it through your fingers is the best way).

Sprinkle a clean, dry work surface with flour and lightly flour your hands to prevent the dough from sticking. Transfer the risen dough to the floured surface and punch it down. Divide the dough into 12 equal pieces and shape each piece into a ball. Flatten each ball of dough to form a disk and, using a floured rolling pin, roll out each disk to a round about 6 inches in diameter and ¹/₈ inch thick. Transfer the rounds to the prepared baking sheets without crowding them.

Place 1 tablespoon or more of the meat mixture on each dough round and spread it almost to the edges. Bake for 10 minutes, or until the edges of the pastries start to turn golden. Sprinkle on the pine nuts and pomegranate seeds and continue baking until the meat is thoroughly cooked (it should no longer be pink) and the edges of the pastries are brown, about 5 minutes longer.

Arrange on a serving platter and serve warm.

# Veal Scaloppine in Port and Pomegranate Sauce

*Gabriel Shachar, head chef of the famed King David Hotel in Jerusalem,*
*created the original recipe. My culinary guru Nizza Ben Shalom of Tel Aviv's Boccaccio*
*Restaurant developed this easy version for the home cook. Serve with any rice dish*
*or Rum and Sweet Potato Purée with Pomegranate Pecans (page 54).*

---

1½ pounds veal scaloppine

Salt and freshly ground black pepper

All-purpose flour, for dredging

1 tablespoon unsalted butter

1 tablespoon olive oil

4 cloves garlic, sliced

1 teaspoon Worcestershire sauce

⅓ cup port

¼ cup Pomegranate Syrup (page 15)

1 teaspoon chopped fresh rosemary leaves

⅓ cup pomegranate seeds

Serves 4

Preheat the oven to 200°F. Pound the veal slices to about ⅛ inch thick. Sprinkle with salt and pepper and dredge both sides in flour.

Melt the butter with the olive oil in a skillet over high heat. Add the floured veal slices in batches (do not crowd them) and fry quickly on both sides. Transfer the fried batches to an oven-proof plate and keep warm in the oven while frying the remaining veal.

When all the veal has been fried and transferred to the oven, add the garlic, Worcestershire sauce, port, pomegranate syrup, and rosemary to the skillet. Stir and cook for 1 to 2 minutes. Taste and adjust the seasoning if needed. Return the veal slices to the skillet for 1 minute—just to take on the flavor of the sauce—and transfer the veal to a serving platter.

Add the pomegranate seeds to the skillet and swirl them around so that they absorb some of the flavor of the sauce. Pour the sauce and seeds over the veal. Serve immediately.

# Lamb Stew with Dried Fruit, Chestnuts, and Pomegranate Syrup

*I realize that a cookbook author shouldn't admit to favorites, but I can't resist this exquisite lamb dish. The fruit, the chestnuts, the pomegranate syrup—all join up with tender lamb to create heaven on a plate!*

---

$1/_4$ cup olive oil

2 yellow onions, chopped

5 cloves garlic, sliced

3 pounds lamb stew, cut into 2-inch cubes

1 teaspoon salt

1 teaspoon freshly ground black pepper

$1/_2$ teaspoon ground turmeric

3 carrots, peeled and cut in thirds on the diagonal

1 leek, white part only, sliced

1 cup beef stock, or 1 bouillon cube dissolved in 1 cup water

1 cup dry red wine

3 tablespoons tomato paste

2 tablespoons balsamic vinegar

$1/_2$ teaspoon ground cinnamon

$1/_2$ teaspoon dried thyme

Grated zest of $1/_2$ lemon

$3/_4$ cup dried apricots

$3/_4$ cup prunes, pitted

$1/_4$ cup Pomegranate Syrup (page 15)

1 cup chestnuts, roasted and shelled

Serves 6 to 8

Heat the olive oil in a Dutch oven over medium heat. Add the onions and garlic and sauté for 5 minutes. Increase the heat to high and add the lamb, salt, pepper, and turmeric. Brown the lamb on all sides.

Add the carrots, leek, stock, wine, tomato paste, vinegar, cinnamon, thyme, and lemon zest. Bring to a boil, decrease the heat to low, cover, and cook for 45 minutes. Add the apricots, prunes, and pomegranate syrup. Stir well, cover, and cook for 30 minutes longer. Add the chestnuts, cover, and cook for 15 minutes longer. The lamb should be tender and the vegetables, soft but not mushy.

# Grilled Beef Fillet with Caramelized Shallot, Marsala, and Pomegranate Marmalade

*For a spectacular summer lunch, serve it with roasted baby potatoes and a salad of mixed greens and red onion dressed with Basic Vinaigrette with Pomegranate Syrup (page 19).*

3 pounds fillet of beef

1 (750-ml) bottle Marsala wine

4 tablespoons olive oil

12 shallots, peeled and thinly sliced

2 tablespoons Pomegranate Syrup (page 15)

1 head of garlic, cloves peeled and minced

Serves 6 to 8

Place the beef fillet in a large nonreactive dish and pour in the entire bottle of Marsala, making sure that all the meat is covered with the wine. Cover the dish, refrigerate, and marinate for 4 to 6 hours. Remove the fillet from the marinade 1 hour before grilling and reserve the marinade.

Heat 2 tablespoons of the olive oil in a large nonstick skillet over medium heat. Add the shallots and sauté for 2 to 4 minutes, just until they become translucent, and then stir in the reserved marinade and the pomegranate syrup. Increase the heat to high, bring to a boil, then decrease the heat to medium-low and cook, stirring frequently, for 30 to 45 minutes, until the liquid is reduced by two-thirds.

Preheat a gas grill to high heat. Combine the minced garlic with the remaining 2 tablespoons of olive oil in a small bowl and blend together well. Rub the beef fillet with the garlic mixture, covering the entire surface.

Grill the fillet over a high flame for 2 minutes on each side to seal the juices. Decrease the flame to medium and grill for 15 to 20 minutes, until medium-rare, turning once at the halfway point. The meat should be browned on the edges and slightly pink inside.

Transfer the fillet to a cutting board and leave the grill on medium heat. Cut the fillet into 1-inch-thick slices. Return the slices to the grill for a few seconds on each side to seal them. Remove the slices before they char. Serve immediately with the Marsala marmalade.

# Seared Salmon Fillets
# with Pomegranate Sherry Glaze

*I don't mind admitting that the inspiration here came from an experiment
in color—the great taste was a bonus.*

---

2 tablespoons sesame oil

6 (1-inch-thick) salmon fillets, with skin on

1/4 cup white wine

3 teaspoons soy sauce

Salt and freshly ground black pepper

2/3 cup freshly squeezed orange juice

1/3 cup pomegranate juice

3 tablespoons sherry

1/4 cup chopped fresh basil leaves

1 teaspoon orange zest

1/2 teaspoon peeled and grated fresh ginger

3/4 cup pomegranate seeds

Fresh mint leaves, for garnish

Serves 6

Preheat the oven to 400°F.

Heat the sesame oil in a skillet over very high heat. Add the salmon fillets and sear quickly, turning once, for about 1 minute on each side. Remove from the heat and transfer to a baking pan.

Combine the wine and soy sauce in a small bowl and season to taste with salt and pepper. Drizzle over the salmon fillets and bake for 10 minutes.

In a small saucepan over medium-high heat, stir together the orange juice, pomegranate juice, sherry, basil, orange zest, and ginger. Cook until the liquid is reduced by half and thickened to a sauce. Add half of the pomegranate seeds, stir, and cook for 1 minute longer. Remove from the heat.

Divide the ramaining pomegranate seeds among the individual plates (add more, if desired) and place the salmon fillets on top. Drizzle with the sauce and garnish with the fresh mint leaves.

# Tuna, Asparagus, and Pomegranate Stir-Fry

*Consider serving the stir-fry atop rice stick or cellophane noodles, or alongside the Couscous, Peanut, and Pomegranate Salad (page 59).*

Sauce

6 tablespoons rice vinegar

3 tablespoons sherry

2 tablespoons Pomegranate Syrup (page 15)

2 tablespoons light soy sauce

1 tablespoon sesame oil

1 tablespoon peeled and grated fresh ginger

2 cloves garlic, minced


1 bunch (about 15 spears) asparagus

$^1/_2$ cup water

3 to 4 tablespoons vegetable oil

1 pound tuna steak, cut into 1-inch chunks

1 (8-ounce) can whole water chestnuts, drained and halved

1 red bell pepper, cut into 2-inch long strips

1 tablespoon unsalted butter

$^1/_3$ cup pomegranate seeds

$^1/_4$ cup sesame seeds, for garnish


Serves 2

Combine the vinegar, sherry, pomegranate syrup, soy sauce, sesame oil, ginger, and garlic in a saucepan over medium heat. Stir and cook for about 5 minutes, or until it is reduced by half and thickened to a sauce. Set aside.

Snap off and discard the tough ends of the asparagus. Cut the spears on the diagonal into 3-inch pieces. Bring the water to a boil in a skillet over high heat and add the asparagus. Decrease the heat, cover, and cook for 3 minutes. Using tongs or a slotted spoon, transfer the asparagus to a plate and set aside.

Heat 3 tablespoons of the corn oil in a wok or a deep skillet. Add the tuna and stir-fry for about 1 minute on each side, just until the tuna changes color and the center is still pink. Transfer the tuna to a plate and keep warm. Add the asparagus, water chestnuts, bell pepper, and the remaining 1 tablespoon of corn oil if needed and stir-fry for 1 minute. Stir in the sauce, butter, and half of the pomegranate seeds and cook for 3 minutes. Return the tuna to the wok, stir for a few seconds, and then remove the wok from the heat.

Distribute the tuna and vegetables among individual plates. Sprinkle with the remaining pomegranate seeds and sesame seeds and serve immediately.

# Shrimp in Brandy and Pomegranate Cream Sauce

*Rice pilaf would make a great accompaniment to this shrimp.*
*But all you really need for the ultimate taste treat is a fresh loaf of crusty bread.*
*You'll want to sop up every bit of this creamy sauce.*

1 tablespoon unsalted butter

2 pounds shrimp, peeled and deveined

3 green onions, white and green parts, sliced

Salt and freshly ground black pepper

$^1/_4$ cup white wine

1 tablespoon brandy

6 cloves garlic, sliced

$^1/_4$ cup whipping cream

2 tablespoons Pomegranate Syrup (page 15)

1 tablespoon chopped fresh basil leaves

1 tablespoon chopped fresh flat-leaf parsley leaves

$^1/_4$ teaspoon red pepper flakes

1 teaspoon freshly squeezed lemon juice

1 lemon, cut into wedges, for garnish

$^1/_2$ teaspoon dried red chile flakes, for garnish (optional)

Serves 4

Melt the butter in a skillet over high heat. Add the shrimp and green onions and season with salt and black pepper. Stir in the wine, brandy, and garlic. Cook for 2 minutes, or just until the shrimp turn pink on both sides (this will happen quickly). Using a slotted spoon, transfer the shrimp to a plate. Set aside and keep warm.

Add the cream, pomegranate syrup, basil, parsley, and red pepper flakes to the skillet. Cook for 1 to 2 minutes to reduce the sauce. Stir in the lemon juice. Return the shrimp to the skillet, stir briefly, and taste and adjust the seasoning. Garnish with lemon wedges and chile flakes before serving.

Blood Orange and Red Grapefruit Sorbets with
Pomegranate and Campari

Pomegranate Poached Quince

Cannoli Cream Pie with Pomegranate Topping
and Chocolate Shavings

White and Dark Chocolate Mousse with Pomegranates

Raspberry and Pomegranate Fool

Rice Pudding with Currants, Pistachios, and Pomegranates

Napoleon with Vanilla Cream, Strawberries, and
Mixed Berry and Pomegranate Coulis

Lemon Mascarpone Tarts with Cornmeal Rosemary Crust
and Pomegranate Topping

Panna Cotta with Mixed Berry and Pomegranate Coulis

Pomegranate Fruit Shake

Pomegranate Sunrise

Pomegranate Royale

Pomegranate Sea Breeze

Orange, Campari, and Pomegranate Slush

Pomegranate Campari

Pomegranate Margarita

# Blood Orange and Red Grapefruit Sorbets
# with Pomegranate and Campari

*Oh, how the simple things in life turn out to be the sweetest! A few basic ingredients, some minor kitchen effort, and you will never go back to store-bought sorbet again. Serve a scoop of each flavor garnished with fresh mint leaves or pomegranate seeds scattered on top.*

---

Blood Orange Sorbet

5 small blood oranges, peeled and pith
    removed

3/4 cup sugar

2 cups pomegranate juice

6 tablespoons Campari

3/4 cup freshly squeezed lemon juice


Red Grapefruit Sorbet

4 red grapefruits, peeled and pith removed

3/4 cup sugar

1 cup pomegranate juice

1/4 cup Campari

1/4 cup freshly squeezed lemon juice


Fresh mint leaves, for garnish

Makes about 5 cups of each sorbet

To make each sorbet, follow the same directions: Cut the citrus fruit into chunks, discarding any seeds, and place in a food processor fitted with the steel blade. Add the sugar and purée. Add the pomegranate juice, Campari, and lemon juice and purée again until smooth.

Transfer the mixture to an ice-cream maker and follow the manufacturer's directions. (Or transfer the mixture to a freezerproof container, cover, and freeze for at least 10 hours.)

When ready to serve, cut the frozen sorbet into chunks and place in a food processor fitted with the steel blade. (If not using all the sorbet at once, process only the amount needed and refreeze the rest immediately.) Purée until the mixture turns creamy. Scoop and serve garnished with fresh mint leaves.

# Pomegranate Poached Quince

*What could be more appropriate than the pairing of two ancient fruits? Quince is the
quintessential dessert throughout the Middle Eastern and Mediterranean regions.
In Turkey, it's served with kaymak—a rich, thick cream—but it's just as lovely with a
dollop of whipped cream, crème fraîche, or sweetened mascarpone.*

---

2 large quinces

3 to 4 cups pomegranate juice

$^1/_2$ cup sugar

Serves 4

Wash the quinces well but do not peel them. Remove the blackened ends
and slice the quinces from stem to end. Leave the cores and pits intact.

Place the quince halves in a wide saucepan, cut side down, one next to
another. To determine how much poaching liquid is needed, pour in the
pomegranate juice to cover. Remove the quince and set aside. Stir the
sugar into the juice. Set over medium heat and bring to a boil. Return the
quince halves cut side down to the pan, decrease the heat to low, and
cover. Simmer for 30 to 60 minutes, depending on the freshness and size
of the fruit. Quince is done when tender and easily pierced with the point
of a knife.

Transfer the quince halves to a cutting board, let cool, and then cut out
the cores. Return the cores to the pan and boil over high heat with the
remaining liquid until it is reduced and thickened to a syrup.

Serve the quince chilled or at room temperature, drizzled with its syrup.

# Cannoli Cream Pie with Pomegranate Topping and Chocolate Shavings

*The inspiration came from my love of cannoli: What if I replaced the traditional candied fruit with pomegranate seeds, added chocolate for pure hedonistic pleasure, and dolloped the whole thing into a ready-made pie shell to make life easy— wouldn't it be amazing? The answer was yes!*

---

1 1/2 cups ricotta cheese

3/4 cup cream cheese, at room temperature

1/2 cup sugar

1/3 cup apricot preserves

1 1/4 cups pomegranate seeds

1 (9-inch) ready-made piecrust (thawed if frozen)

1/3 cup Pomegranate Syrup (page 15)

1 (3 1/2-ounce) bittersweet chocolate bar

Serves 6

In a blender or a food processor fitted with the plastic blade, combine the ricotta, cream cheese, sugar, and apricot preserves. Blend just enough to combine; do not overmix. Transfer to a bowl and fold in 1/2 cup of the pomegranate seeds. Cover and refrigerate to chill.

Bake the piecrust according to the package directions and let cool. Pour the chilled cheese mixture into the cooled piecrust and smooth the top.

Combine the remaining pomegranate seeds and syrup in a bowl. Stir well and spread it over the top of the pie.

Using a vegetable peeler, shave the chocolate bar over the pie. Cover with plastic wrap and refrigerate to chill for 4 hours.

*Variation: Use 6 individual chocolate cups in place of the piecrust and chocolate shavings. Pour the cheese filling into the chocolate cups and spread with the pomegranate topping.*

# White and Dark Chocolate Mousse with Pomegranates

*Yes, it's a lot of effort. But if you keep the rest of the meal simple, this dessert will knock 'em out. Try mixing pomegranate seeds into the white chocolate mousse for a festive presentation.*

5 ounces white chocolate

5 ounces bittersweet chocolate

$^1/_2$ cup (1 stick) unsalted butter, at room temperature

6 egg yolks

3 tablespoons sugar

1 cup whipping cream

3 egg whites

1 teaspoon Cointreau or orange-flavored liqueur

1/3 cup pomegranate seeds

1 cup Pomegranate Syrup (page 15)

Serves 8

Make each chocolate mousse separately: Melt the white chocolate in the top of a double boiler over (but not touching) simmering water. Add $^1/_4$ cup of the butter and stir well. Transfer the white chocolate mixture to a bowl and set aside. Repeat the process with the bittersweet chocolate.

Using an electric mixer, beat the egg yolks with 1 tablespoon of the sugar. Heat the yolk mixture in the top of a double boiler over (but not touching) simmering water, stirring for about 5 minutes, until the mixture thickens. Remove from the heat and let it cool slightly. Divide the yolk mixture equally between the two chocolate mixtures and stir it in.

Beat the cream until stiff peaks form. Divide the whipped cream equally between the two chocolate mixtures and fold it in.

Beat the egg whites until they start to stiffen. Beat in the remaining 2 tablespoons of sugar. Divide the egg white mixture equally between the two chocolate mixtures and gently fold it in.

Stir the Cointreau into the dark chocolate mousse. Select 8 parfait glasses and drop 1 teaspoon of pomegranate seeds into each glass. Fill a pastry bag with the dark chocolate mousse and squeeze it into each glass, filling it halfway. Drop another teaspoon of pomegranate seeds onto the dark chocolate mousse layer. Fill a pastry bag with the white chocolate mousse and squeeze it onto the pomegranate seeds to fill the glass. Drizzle 1 tablespoon of the pomegranate syrup over each parfait and sprinkle with the remaining pomegranate seeds. Cover and refrigerate until ready to serve.

# Raspberry and Pomegranate Fool

*Hot pink ribboning through all that white and pink fluff is gorgeous. If you have amaretto cookies on hand, crush them and sprinkle over the fools for a special touch.*

2 cups (10 ounces) frozen raspberries

1/4 cup pomegranate juice

2 tablespoons Pomegranate Syrup (page 15)

3 tablespoons Cointreau or Grand Marnier

1/4 cup pomegranate seeds

1 cup whipping cream

2 tablespoons sugar

Serves 6

In a small saucepan over medium heat, stir together the frozen raspberries, pomegranate juice, and pomegranate syrup. Cook, stirring constantly, until it just starts to bubble. Smash the raspberries with the back of a spoon, so that they lose their shape and the sauce becomes chunky. Remove from the heat and stir in the Cointreau and pomegranate seeds. Set aside 1/2 cup of the raspberry sauce and transfer the rest to a large bowl.

Beat the cream until soft peaks form. Add the sugar and continue beating until stiff peaks form. Gently fold the whipped cream into the raspberry sauce but do not fully blend.

Spoon the cream mixture into 6 martini òr parfait glasses and refrigerate to chill. When ready to serve, drizzle with the reserved sauce. (Or layer the raspberry sauce between scoops of the raspberry whipped cream.)

# Rice Pudding with Currants, Pistachios, and Pomegranates

*The classic, creamy comfort food gets an exotic twist with the addition of crunchy pistachios and pomegranate seeds bursting with juice. If you have one, a thermometer is helpful for testing to determine that perfect moment when the pudding is ready.*

²/₃ cup medium- or short-grain white rice

4³/₄ cups milk

¹/₃ cup sugar

2 tablespoons unsalted butter, at room temperature

Pinch of salt

¹/₄ cup toasted pistachios, chopped (see note, page 31)

¹/₃ cup currants

2 teaspoons vanilla extract

2 egg yolks

¹/₃ cup pomegranate seeds

Serves 6

Soak the rice for 10 minutes and rinse in a sieve several times until the water runs clear. In a heavy saucepan over medium-low heat, combine 4 cups of the milk, the rice, sugar, butter, and salt. Simmer for about 1 hour, stirring frequently so that the rice at the bottom of the pan does not burn. When all the liquid is absorbed and the rice is softened, creamy, and a bit chunky, remove from the heat. Stir in the pistachios, currants, and vanilla.

Heat the remaining ³/₄ cup milk in a small saucepan over medium heat. Bring to a simmer and remove from the heat. Beat the egg yolks in a bowl and gradually whisk the heated milk into the yolks. Return the mixture to the saucepan over medium heat and cook for 3 to 5 minutes. Do not let the mixture come to a boil. Remove from the heat when a thermometer inserted into the liquid reads 160°F.

Stir the egg mixture into the rice mixture, combine well, and let cool slightly. Stir in the pomegranate seeds. Spoon the mixture into 6 ramekins. Place the ramekins on a baking sheet, cover with waxed paper, and refrigerate until ready to serve.

# Napoleon with Vanilla Cream, Strawberries, and Mixed Berry and Pomegranate Coulis

*If there is a better ménage a trois than a sweet, crunchy layer of pastry topped with mounds of vanilla cream and drizzled with a fruit-laden sauce, I've yet to discover it.*

Pastry

16 ounces puff pastry dough (thawed if frozen)

2 tablespoons unsalted butter, melted

$1/2$ cup sugar

Vanilla Cream

1 cup milk

1 cup whipping cream

1 (3-ounce) package instant vanilla pudding mix

1 teaspoon vanilla extract

1 cup sliced fresh strawberries

1 cup pomegranate seeds

1 recipe Mixed Berry and Pomegranate Coulis (pages 18-19)

Serves 4 (or 6)

Preheat the oven to 500°F.

Sprinkle a clean work surface with flour. Roll out the puff pastry dough to the size of the baking sheet and $1/8$ inch thick. Transfer to the baking sheet. Brush the entire surface of the dough with the melted butter and sprinkle with the sugar. Score the dough lengthwise and crosswise to form 12 equal squares. Refrigerate the baking sheet until the oven is fully heated.

When ready to bake, cover the dough surface with a sheet of parchment paper. Set another, slightly smaller baking sheet on top to weigh it down. (This prevents the dough from puffing up during baking.) Bake for about 20 minutes, or until it turns golden. Transfer to a rack and let cool. Cut the cooled pastry into squares along the score lines and set aside.

Combine the milk, cream, vanilla pudding mix, and vanilla extract in a bowl. Using an electric mixer, beat on high speed until frothy.

Place 1 pastry square on each plate. Top with a dollop of the vanilla cream, a few strawberry slices, some pomegranate seeds, and a drizzling of the coulis. Repeat to make a second layer and top with another pastry square (or use only 2 pastry squares per napoleon and serve 6). Drizzle more coulis around the plate.

# Lemon Mascarpone Tarts with Cornmeal Rosemary Crust and Pomegranate Topping

*The mascarpone adds a luscious creamy texture; the cornmeal and rosemary crust, a bit of surprise, and the pomegranate seeds—as always—are mesmerizing to look at, delectable to eat. If the task seems daunting, forgo the crust and use ready-made pie shells—but don't change another thing!*

---

### Filling

Grated zest and juice of 3 lemons

1 cup sugar

$^1/_2$ cup (1 stick) unsalted butter, at room temperature

3 large eggs, beaten

$^3/_4$ cup whipping cream

$^3/_4$ cup mascarpone cheese

### Crust

3 cups all-purpose flour

1 cup cornmeal

$^1/_4$ cup sugar

$^1/_2$ teaspoon salt

1 cup (2 sticks) unsalted butter, at room temperature, cut in small pieces

4 teaspoons finely chopped fresh rosemary leaves

6 to 10 tablespoons ice water

Make the filling 1 day in advance: Combine the lemon zest, lemon juice, sugar, and butter in the top of a double boiler over (but not touching) simmering water. Stir constantly, until the butter and sugar are completely dissolved. Add the eggs and cook, stirring constantly, for about 6 minutes, or until the mixture is thickened to the consistency of heavy cream. (Do not let it come to a boil.) Remove from the heat, strain the mixture through a fine-mesh sieve into a heatproof bowl, and let cool. Place a layer of plastic wrap directly on the surface of the lemon cream (to prevent a skin from forming) and refrigerate overnight.

To make the crust, combine the flour, cornmeal, sugar, and salt in a food processor fitted with the steel blade. Pulse until combined. Add the butter pieces and rosemary and continue pulsing until the mixture is mealy. Drizzle in the ice water 1 tablespoon at a time, just until the mixture comes together. You should be able to squeeze a handful together. If the dough crumbles, add a bit more water. Divide the dough in half and form each half into a ball. Wrap in plastic wrap and refrigerate for at least 1 hour.

Preheat the oven to 375°F.

Topping

$1/2$ cup Pomegranate Syrup (page 15)

2 to 3 cups pomegranate seeds

Makes 2 (9-inch) tarts, or 16 (4-inch) tartlets

Remove the dough balls from the refrigerator and let stand at room temperature for 15 minutes. Sprinkle a clean work surface and a rolling pin with flour. Working with one ball of dough at a time, roll out each ball to a round 12 inches in diameter and $1/4$ inch thick. (For individual tartlets, use a cookie cutter or small bowl to cut out rounds 2 inches larger than the diameter of the tartlet pans.) Transfer the dough into the pans, trim away the excess from the top, and pierce the center a few times with a knifepoint or toothpick. Bake for 20 to 30 minutes, until the center and sides turn golden. Transfer to a rack to cool.

Using an electric mixer, beat the cream until it starts to stiffen, and then slowly add in the mascarpone. Beat just until well blended. Fold into the chilled lemon mixture. Pour the filling into the prebaked tart shells and smooth the tops.

To make the topping, pour the pomegranate syrup into a bowl and stir in the pomegranate seeds, using more or less according to taste. (The syrup helps bind the seeds together, but you can omit the syrup and just spoon on the seeds.) Carefully spoon the mixture onto the tops of the lemon tarts. Cover with plastic wrap and refrigerate until ready to serve.

# Panna Cotta with Mixed Berry and Pomegranate Coulis

*Is any collection of desserts complete without at least one reference to the Italians? Making this custard was a lot easier than I had predicted, and having the Mixed Berry and Pomegranate Coulis on hand meant that I could whip up the whole thing the same day company was expected.*

---

1 cup milk

1 tablespoon (1 envelope) unflavored gelatin

2 cups whipping cream

$^1/_2$ cup sugar

1$^1/_2$ teaspoons vanilla extract

1 cup Mixed Berry and Pomegranate Coulis (pages 18-19)

$^1/_2$ cup pomegranate seeds, for garnish

Serves 8

Pour $^1/_2$ cup of the milk into a small saucepan and sprinkle with the gelatin. Let stand for 3 minutes to soften. Set over low heat and cook, stirring constantly, for 2 to 3 minutes, until the gelatin is dissolved.

Stir in the remaining $^1/_2$ cup of milk, the cream, sugar, and vanilla. Increase the heat to medium and cook just until it starts to steam. (This takes only a few minutes—do not let it boil!) Remove from the heat, cover the pan, and let stand for about 15 minutes.

Pour the mixture into 8 ramekins. Cover with plastic wrap and refrigerate for at least 5 hours.

When ready to serve, set each ramekin in a shallow bowl of hot water for 2 to 3 seconds. Slide a knife around the edge of the panna cotta to loosen it from the dish. Cover with a plate and invert—the panna cotta should slip right out. (Tap with the back of a spoon if necessary.) Spoon the berry and pomegranate coulis on top of the panna cotta. Garnish with the pomegranate seeds.

# Pomegranate Fruit Shake

*Go ahead; it's good for you and delicious!*

---

1 banana, sliced

$^1/_2$ cup fresh strawberries, sliced, plus
    $^1/2$ strawberry, for garnish

1 cup milk or yogurt

2 tablespoons Pomegranate Syrup (page 15)

2 tablespoons crushed ice

Serves 1

Combine all the ingredients in a blender and purée until blended and creamy. Pour into a glass and garnish with the strawberry half perched on the rim of the glass.

# Pomegranate Sunrise

*Start the day with a gorgeous Pomegranate Sunrise and what can go wrong after that?*

---

Crushed ice

2 tablespoons pomegranate juice

2 tablespoons freshly squeezed orange juice

2 tablespoons tequila

Serves 1

Fill a glass with crushed ice. Combine the pomegranate juice, orange juice, and tequila in a cocktail shaker. Shake well and pour into the ice-filled glass.

# Pomegranate Royale

*What elegance! Wouldn't Noël Coward have just loved it?*

1 tablespoon Pomegranate Syrup (page 15)

1 tablespoon crème de cassis

$^1/_2$ cup champagne or sparkling wine

Pomegranate seeds, for garnish

Serves 1

Combine the pomegranate syrup and crème de cassis in a champagne flute and stir. Pour in the champagne and drop in a few pomegranate seeds.


# Pomegranate Sea Breeze

*Think beach, bar, and a gentle sea breeze.*

Ice cubes

2 tablespoons vodka

2 tablespoons cranberry juice

1 tablespoon freshly squeezed grapefruit juice

1 tablespoon pomegranate juice

1 tablespoon Pomegranate Syrup (page 15)

1 lime peel twist

Serves 1

Fill a highball glass with ice. Pour in the vodka, cranberry juice, grapefruit juice, pomegranate juice, and pomegranate syrup. Stir well and garnish with the lime twist.

# Orange, Campari, and Pomegranate Slush

*Ah, the joy of it! Keep the sorbet in the freezer and multiply this recipe to whip up a batch of slurpy slushes for family and friends.*

---

¹/₂ cup Blood Orange Sorbet with Pomegranate and Campari (page 90)

1 tablespoon Pomegranate Syrup (page 15)

¹/₄ cup seltzer or sparkling water

Pomegranate seeds, for garnish

Serves 1

Combine the sorbet and pomegranate syrup in a blender and process until slushy. Pour into a glass and add the seltzer.

Garnish with pomegranate seeds dropped on top.

# Pomegranate Campari

*Perfect for Sunday brunch or an evening cocktail, the combination of Campari and pomegranate juice can't be beat.*

---

¹/₂ cup pomegranate juice

2 teaspoons confectioners' sugar

¹/₄ cup Campari

4 ice cubes

2 lemon slices

Serves 1

Pour the pomegranate juice into a glass, add the confectioners' sugar, and stir well. Pour in the Campari and add the ice cubes.

Drop in the lemon slices.

# Pomegranate Margarita

*It was only a matter of time before the pomegranate ended up as the star ingredient in this classic cocktail.*

---

### Frost

$^1/_2$ cup pomegranate juice

$^1/_2$ cup coarse salt

### Drink

2 tablespoons Pomegranate Syrup (page 15)

2 tablespoons tequila

2 tablespoons Cointreau

1 tablespoon freshly squeezed lime juice

1 tablespoon sugar syrup (see note)

2 ice cubes

Serves 1

To make a frosted edge on the glass, invert the glass into a bowl of pomegranate juice to wet the rim. Prepare a plate of salt and dip the wet edge of the glass into it. Move it around until the entire rim is coated.

In a small pitcher, combine the pomegranate syrup, tequila, Cointreau, lime juice, and sugar syrup and stir until blended. Pour into the prepared margarita glass and add the ice cubes. Garnish with a twist of lime, if desired.

For a frozen version, combine all ingredients in a blender and process until blended and frothy. Pour into a prepared margarita glass.

*Note: Sugar syrup is easy to make and great to have on hand. Combine equal parts of water and sugar in a saucepan over medium heat (or use a microwave oven). Cook, stirring, until the sugar is completely dissolved. Store in a sealed jar in the refrigerator.*

# Index

Almonds
  Chilled Melon and Mint Soup with Pomegranates and Toasted, 43
  Parsley Salad with Feta, and Pomegranates, 56, **57**
Antipasti in Pomegranate Balsamic Dressing, 26
Apricots
  Duck Breasts in, Shallot, and Pomegranate Sauce, 72, **73**
  Jeweled Rice with Pistachios, and Pomegranates, 58
  Lamb Stew with Dried Fruit, Chestnuts, and Pomegranate Syrup, 79
Asparagus, Tuna, and Pomegranate Stir-Fry, **84**, 85
Avocados
  Celebration Salad with Pomegranate Poppy Seed Dressing, 47
  Endive, and Grapefruit Salad, **48–49**, 49
  Pomegranate Guacamole, 30

Bacon-Wrapped Chicken Roll-ups with Goat Cheese in Pomegranate Cream Sauce, 67
Baharat, 36
Basic Vinaigrette with Pomegranate Juice, 18
Basic Vinaigrette with Pomegranate Syrup, 19
Beef, Grilled Fillet with Caramelized Shallot, Marsala, and Pomegranate Marmalade, 80, **81**
Beet and Pomegranate Borscht, 38, **39**
Berries
  Mixed Berry and Pomegranate Coulis, 19

Napoleon with Vanilla Cream, Strawberries, and Mixed Berry and Pomegranate Coulis, 98, **99**
Panna Cotta with Mixed Berry and Pomegranate Coulis, **102**, 103
Blood Orange and Red Grapefruit Sorbets with Pomegranate and Campari, 90, **91**
Blue Cheese, Grilled Haloumi, and Pomegranate Salad, 52, **53**
Borscht, Beet and Pomegranate, 38, **39**
Bruschetta with Goat Cheese, Red Onion, and Pomegranate Salsa, **32**, 33
Bulghur, Pomegranate Tabbouleh, 62

Campari
  Blood Orange and Red Grapefruit Sorbets with Pomegranate and, 90, **91**
  Orange, and Pomegranate Slush, 106
  Pomegranate, 106, **107**
Cannoli Cream Pie with Pomegranate Topping and Chocolate Shavings, 93
Celebration Salad with Pomegranate Poppy Seed Dressing, 47
Cheese. *See* Blue Cheese; Feta Cheese; Goat Cheese; Haloumi Cheese; Mascarpone Cheese; Ricotta Cheese; Roquefort Cheese
Chestnuts, Lamb Stew with Dried Fruit, and Pomegranate Syrup, 79
Chicken
  Bacon-Wrapped, Roll-ups with Goat Cheese in Pomegranate Cream Sauce, 67
  Curried, Salad with Grapes, Pecans, and Pomegranates, 50
  In Root Vegetable, Pomegranate, and Dried Fruit Sauce, **68**, 69

Walnut, Date, and Pomegranate, 66
Chilled Melon and Mint Soup with Pomegranates and Toasted Almonds, **42**, 43
Chocolate
  Cannoli Cream Pie with Pomegranate Topping and, Shavings, 93
  White and Dark, Mousse with Pomegranates, 94, **95**
Cornish Hen, Stuffed, with Orange Pomegranate Glaze, 70–71
Coulis
  Mixed Berry and Pomegranate, 19
  Napoleon with Vanilla Cream, Strawberries, and Mixed Berry and Pomegranate, 98, **99**
  Panna Cotta with Mixed Berry and Pomegranate, **102**, 103
Couscous, Peanut, and Pomegranate Salad, 59
Cranberries, Kumquat, and Pomegranate Relish, 28, **29**
Cucumbers, Yogurt Soup with Pomegranates and Mint, 41, **42**
Currants, Rice Pudding with, Pistachios, and Pomegranates, 97
Curried Chicken Salad with Grapes, Pecans, and Pomegranates, 50

Dates, Walnut, and Pomegranate Chicken, 66
Dips, Red Pepper, Walnut, and Pomegranate, 31, **32**
Duck Breasts in Apricot, Shallot, and Pomegranate Sauce, 72, **73**

Endive, Avocado, and Grapefruit Salad, **48–49**, 49
Feta Cheese
Parsley Salad with, Almonds, and Pomegranates, 56, **57**
Quinoa Salad with Herbs, and Pomegranates, **60**, 61
Figs, Drunken, with Roquefort in Pomegranate Syrup, 23

Goat Cheese
Bacon-Wrapped Chicken Roll-ups with, in Pomegranate Cream Sauce, 67
Bruschetta with, Red Onion, and Pomegranate, **32**, 33

Grilled Pear, and Pomegranate Salad, 46
Grapefruit
Blood Orange and Red, Sorbets with Pomegranate and Campari, 90, **91**
Celebration Salad with Pomegranate Poppy Seed Dressing, 47
Endive, Avocado, and, Salad, **48–49**, 49
Grape Leaves, Stuffed, in Tomato Pomegranate Sauce, 36–37
Grapes, Curried Chicken Salad with, Pecans, and Pomegranates, 50
Grilled Beef Fillet with Caramelized Shallot, Marsala, and Pomegranate Marmalade, 80, **81**
Grilled Haloumi, Blue Cheese, and Pomegranate Salad, 52, **53**
Grilled Pear, Goat Cheese, and Pomegranate Salad, 46
Ground Beef
Meat, Pine Nut, and Pomegranate Pastries, 76–77, **77**
Stuffed Squash in Tomato Pomegranate Sauce, 74
Guacamole, Pomegranate, 30

Haloumi Cheese
Grilled Haloumi, Blue Cheese, and Pomegranate Salad, 52, **53**
Haloumi, Tapenade, and Pomegranate Bites, 24, **25**
Herb and Pomegranate Soup, 40

Jeweled Rice with Pistachios, Apricots, and Pomegranates, 58

Kumquat, Cranberry, and Pomegranate Relish, 28, **29**

Lamb Stew with Dried Fruit, Chestnuts, and Pomegranate Syrup, 79
Lemon Mascarpone Tarts with Corneal Rosemary Crust and Pomegranate Topping, 100–101

Mango, Pepper, and Pomegranate Salsa, 27
Mascarpone Cheese, Lemon Mascarpone Tarts with Corneal, Rosemary Crust and Pomegranate Topping, 100–101
Meat, Pine Nut, and Pomegranate Pastries, 76–77, 77
Melon, Chilled, and Mint Soup with Pomegranates and Toasted, 43
Mint, Chilled Melon and, Soup with Pomegranates and Toasted, 43
Mixed Berry and Pomegranate Coulis, 19
Molasses, Pomegranate, 16, 17
Mousse, White and Dark Chocolate, with Pomegranates, 94, 95

Napoleon with Vanilla Cream, Strawberries, and Mixed Berry and Pomegranate Coulis, 98, **99**

Nuts. *See also* Almonds; Peanuts; Pecans; Pistachios; Walnuts
toasted, 31

Okra Stew in Tomato Pomegranate Sauce, 55
Olives
Haloumi, Tapenade, and Pomegranate Bites, 24, **25**
Pomegranate Marinated, 22
Oranges
Blood Orange and Red Grapefruit Sorbets with Pomegranate and Campari, 90, **91**
Celebration Salad with Pomegranate Poppy Seed Dressing, 47
Orange, Campari, and Pomegranate Slush, 106
Panna Cotta with Mixed Berry and Pomegranate Coulis, **102**, 103
Parsley Salad with Feta, Almonds, and Pomegranates, 56, **57**
Peanut, Couscous, and Pomegranate Salad, 59
Pears
Grilled, Goat Cheese, and Pomegranate Salad, 46
Grilled Haloumi, Blue Cheese, and Pomegranate Salad, 52, **53**
Pecans
Curried Chicken Salad with Grapes, and Pomegranates, 50
Rum and Sweet Potato Purée with Pomegranate, 54
Wheat Berries with, Raisins, and Pomegranates, 63
Peppers
Mango, and Pomegranate, 27
Red Pepper, Walnut, and Pomegranate Dip, 31
Pies. *See also* Tarts
Cannoli Cream, with Pomegranate Topping and Chocolate Shavings, 93
Pine Nuts, Meat, and Pomegranate Pastries, 76–77, **77**
Pistachios
Jeweled Rice with, Apricots, and Pomegranates, 58

Pistachios, *continued*
  Rice Pudding with Currants, and
    Pomegranates, 97
Pomegranates, 4–9
  artistic images of, 7–8
  Bible references to, 6–7
  in folk medicine, 8
  juicing, 12
  literary references to, 7
  seeding, 13–14
  selecting and storing, 12
Prunes, Lamb Stew with Dried Fruit,
    Chestnuts, and Pomegranate Syrup, 79

Quince, Pomegranate Poached, 92
Quinoa Salad with Herbs, Feta, and
    Pomegranates, **60**, 61

Raisins, Wheat Berries with Pecans, and
    Pomegranates, 63
Raspberry and Pomegranate Fool, 96
Red Pepper, Walnut, and Pomegranate
    Dip, 31
Relishes, Kumquat, Cranberry, and
    Pomegranate, 28, **29**
Rice. *See also* Couscous
  Jeweled, with Pistachios, Apricots, and
    Pomegranates, 58
  Pudding with Currants, Pistachios, and
    Pomegranates, 97
  Seafood, and Pomegranate Salad, 51
  Stuffed Squash in Tomato Pomegranate
    Sauce, 74
Ricotta Cheese, Cannoli Cream Pie with
    Pomegranate Topping and Chocolate
    Shavings
Roquefort Cheese, Drunken Figs with, in
    Pomegranate Syrup
Rum and Sweet Potato Purée with
    Pomegranate Pecans, 54

Salad dressings
  Antipasti in Pomegranate Balsamic
    Dressing, 26
  Basic Vinaigrette, 18–19
Salmon
  Gravlax with Pomegranate Balsamic
    Dressing, **34**, 35
  Seared, Fillets with Pomegranate Sherry
    Glaze, 82, **83**
Salsa
  Bruschetta with Goat Cheese, Red Onion,
    and Pomegranate, **32**, 33
  Mango, Pepper, and Pomegranate, 27
Seafood
  Rice, Seafood, and Pomegranate Salad, 51
  Salmon Gravlax with Pomegranate
    Balsamic Dressing, **34**, 35
  Seared Salmon Fillets with Pomegranate
    Sherry Glaze, 82, **83**
  Shrimp in Brandy and Pomegranate
    Cream Sauce, 86, **87**
  Tuna, Asparagus, and Pomegranate Stir-Fry,
    **84**, 85
Seared Salmon Fillets with Pomegranate
    Sherry Glaze, 82, 83
Shallots
  Duck Breasts in Apricot, and Pomegranate
    Sauce, 72, **73**
  Grilled Beef Fillet with Caramelized,
    Marsala, and Pomegranate Marmalade,
    80, **81**
Shrimp in Brandy and Pomegranate Cream
    Sauce, 86, **87**
Sorbets, Blood Orange and Red Grapefruit,
    with Pomegranate and Campari, 90, **91**
Spareribs in Pomegranate Barbecue
    Sauce, 75
Squash, Stuffed, in Tomato Pomegranate
    Sauce, 74
Stir-Fries, Tuna, Asparagus, and Pomegranate,
    **84**, 85

Strawberries
  Napoleon with Vanilla Cream, and Mixed
    Berry and Pomegranate Coulis, 98, **99**
  Pomegranate Fruit Shake, 104
Stuffed Cornish Hen with Orange
    Pomegranate Glaze, 70–71
Stuffed Grape Leaves in Tomato Pomegranate Sauce, 36–37
Stuffed Squash in Tomato Pomegranate
    Sauce, **73**, 74
Sweet Potatoes
  Antipasti in Pomegranate Balsamic
    Dressing, 26
  Rum and, Purée with Pomegranate
    Pecans, 54
Syrup, Pomegranate, 15

Tabbouleh, Pomegranate, 62
Tapenades, Haloumi, and Pomegranate Bites,
    24, **25**
Tarts. *See also* Pies
  Lemon Mascarpone, with Corneal,
    Rosemary Crust and Pomegranate
    Topping, 100–101
Tuna, Asparagus, and Pomegranate Stir-Fry,
    **84**, 85

Veal Scaloppine in Port and Pomegranate
    Sauce, 78

Walnuts
  Date, and Pomegranate Chicken, 66
  Pomegranate Tabbouleh, 62
  Red Pepper, and Pomegranate Dip, 31
  Wheat Berries with Pecans, Raisins, and
    Pomegranates, 63
  White and Dark Chocolate Mousse with
    Pomegranates, 94, **95**

Yogurt Soup with Pomegranates and
    Mint, 41